"Mend thy speech a little,
lest it mar thy fortunes."

Shakespeare, *King Lear*

Talking Your Way to the Top
Copyright © 2019 John Wareham.
All rights reserved

ISBN: 978-0-9795415-0-6

Flatiron Press, New York

Talking Your Way to the TOP

JOHN WAREHAM

The Nervous Person's Heaven Sent
Overnight Guide to Public Speaking

Illustrated by Anthony Viola

Also by John Wareham:

Novels
Chancey on Top
The President's Therapist

Poetry
Sonnets for Sinners, an anthology
How to Survive a Bullet to the Heart,

Memoir
Exposed

Non Fiction
Secrets of a Corporate Headhunter
Wareham's Way
Wareham's Basic Business Types
The Anatomy of a Great Executive
The New Secrets of a Corporate Headhunter
How to Break Out of Prison

Talking Your Way to the **TOP**

The Nervous Person's Heaven Sent Overnight Guide to Public Speaking

Illustrated by Anthony Viola

John Wareham is principal of Wareham Associates, leadership consultants, and creator of the Eagles Foundation *Taking Wings*® personal development program. He is a national oratory winner, parliamentary debate champion, keynote speaker, and "hands down winner" among business communicators according to the *Financial Times*.

His schooldays memoir, *Exposed: how a lost boy bucked the system and found his voice*, shares his inspiring intellectual and emotional journey from tongue-tied stutterer to public speaking champion.

John has led symposia for corporate leaders throughout the world, and presented the *Taking Wings*® program to prison inmates and 'at-risk' youth.

John also applied the management principles he teaches to ocean racing, skippering his own yacht to win class and division in the 650 mile Sydney to Hobart race.

Corporate: www.wareham.org
Pro Bono: www.eaglegather.org
Authors Guild: www.johnwareham.com

Special thanks to the early critics and supporters who taught me so much about the art of platform presentation, especially Ben O'Connor, who touched so many lives; to all my colleagues and competitors in parliamentary debate, especially my team-members Peter Blizard and Tom Jackson; to the leaders who subsequently attended my seminars, both in and out of prison; to Denis O'Reilly and all Black Power and Mongrel Mob leaders; to my good friend Tony Viola for the aptly brilliant illustrations; to John Weber and my daughter Louise for their sensitive edits; to actor and film maker Gwen O'Donnell for her insightful suggestions. I should also single out Evan Whitton, Ken Bowden and Tim De Werff, all of whom showed me how to fine-tune a message. And, of course, my most special thanks to my wife and lifetime guardian angel, Margaret.

Talking Your Way to the TOP

The Nervous Person's Heaven Sent Overnight Guide to Public Speaking

 HEAVENLY SECRETS

How to Seem a Supernatural Speaker 11

How to Turn Nervous Energy into Charismatic Gold,
    and Deliver the Presentation of Your Life 20

10 Steps to a Sublime PowerPoint Presentation 36

How to Give a Glorious Off-the-Cuff Speech 42

How to Debate Like a Pro
and Become an Omnipotent Advocate in Any Setting 48

How to be Seem Blessed with a Wunderkind Mind 55

How to Run a Miraculous Meeting 58

How to Pitch a Bewitching Question 76

How to Overpower Moguls
    and Deliver Big-Ticket Deals 80

How to Turn a Devilish Delegate
    into an Apostle 84

How to Star on Television 91

Ten Commandments,
    Two Secrets and One Dream 102

How to Seem a Supernatural Speaker

> "We succeed in enterprises which demand our positive qualities, but we excel in those that can also make use of our defects."
> —de Toqueville

I MAY BE DEAD ALREADY. But no matter. Whether it's reaching you from this world or the next, this book is surely heaven sent. Let me explain.

If I expired it happened when I was just eighteen. I was waiting for Godot in my father's car. I'd hooked a hose to the tailpipe and fed it into the cabin. Then I hit the ignition. The engine purred and that sickly sweet scent of carbon monoxide invaded my nostrils. I can't be certain of what happened next, so perhaps I'm enjoying the afterlife.

What I seem to recall, however, is that the car stalled, thereby halting one journey and hurling me into another.

It was the stutter I was born with that prompted me to seek a happier place. As I grew older it got worse. Teenage years were torture. By the time I'd finished asking a girl out on a date she'd gone elsewhere. I seriously contemplated pretending to be mute and restricting all communication to a notepad.

Fortunately, when the car stalled—or seemed to—I saw my impediment in a new light. I must fix it or amount to nothing. Not in this world, anyway.

> *The mere idea of public speaking frightens many people. They make excuses and back away—and the confident life they might have lived is lost.*

I withdrew literally every book on stuttering from the local library. Nobody had a cure. Some said speak deliberately and slowly. Some said buy yourself a metronome or beat time with your foot. Some said take up an outdoor sport. Most said stuttering was a psychological problem, a childish way of getting attention. Some said analyze your dreams. Some said just accept it. But nobody knew anything. Indeed, Sigmund Freud remarked, "The only thing I know about this problem is that it does not respond to psychotherapy."

But I learned something from a therapist whom I saw for a couple of months. When psychoanalysis failed she asked me to read brief passages aloud. I got nowhere and wound up weeping. So then she asked me to "shadow" her words with my own. "I will read," she said, "and you will listen very closely. The moment I speak a word, say it out loud with me—even as you are listening for the next word. We will go on like this for as long as we can." As she began, I listened closely. Then—one word at a time, one clause at a time, one sentence at a time—I followed immediately behind her, fluently and effortlessly right to the end. I was astonished. For the first time in my life, I was reading out loud, perfectly, in the presence of another person. So! My stutter was surmountable.

I decided to read aloud for an hour a day. But in the absence of someone for me to "shadow" I made no progress. So I took to reciting the 107 verses of The Rubaiyat of Omar Khayyam. Like shadow reading, the need to focus upon rhythm distracted me from the act of speaking. If I stayed staccato I was okay. But my everyday speech remained in stutter mode. And fitting Khayyam's wisdom into everyday conversations proved difficult. So I quit my morning exercises and signed up for a ten-session course in public speaking.

I joined an earnest dozen erstwhile public speakers. Our tutor asked each of us to step to the platform, give our names, and read fifty words from a newspaper. My knees shook. My throat went dry. My tongue seemed to swell. And I mouthed words that refused to come. The audience was embarrassed and my tutor chagrined.

I attended every session, but showed scant improvement. I could stumble through a few painful platform minutes, glad not to be among the audience trying to listen.

On the final evening our tutor told of how he'd won the local university's medal for oratory, a coveted prize that attracted aspiring attorneys and politicians.

My tutor was a mousy fellow. If he could win it, so could I. Sure, I still couldn't give a coherent speech. And, yes, students winced whenever I appeared. But I vowed, nonetheless, to win that glittering medal.

> Some people say you should begin with small goals and work up. I've gotten better mileage from big goals. Suddenly, you're playing in the big leagues. Everything is much more exciting and energizing–and easier! Not that you don't experience problems along the way.

Failing to apprehend the extent of my impediment, a well-meaning acquaintance recruited me into a swanky public speaking club. The members—mostly barristers, politicians, and business leaders—all seemed eight feet tall and all delivered confident, eloquent speeches. I was mesmerized.

At the end of that first evening the chairman sought extemporaneous speakers from the floor. Taking on a life of its own, my arm raised itself and attracted the chairman's eye. My legs walked me up onto the stage. My attempt to talk for my allotted sixty seconds was terrible. When my time was up, the audience applauded politely and the chairman made a kind comment. I returned to my seat, where a couple of other erstwhile speakers—who also happened to be office colleagues—said I'd made a fool of myself. Thank goodness they hadn't been so stupid as to step onto that stage, they said.

> *Naysayers are always on hand. I've learned, however, that the apprehension of failure is inevitably worse than failure itself—and that the best way to overcome it, in this life anyway, is just to plunge ahead.*

Because I kept on going back to the meetings, I was put into a B grade debating team (there were only two grades) with two young barristers. They were fine but my tongue-tied efforts wrought our defeat throughout the entire season.

But I was improving! I could make myself understood in everyday life. And, onstage, I could string a few flawless sentences together before stumbling.

As the club year drew to a close, the president announced an important national oratory competition. It would be held in a month and was open to all comers.

Oh happy day! This was something I could surely win. Why did I think that I could string a speech together for twelve minutes—or even fit a twelve-minute speech into twelve minutes? Good question. I just had a strange belief in my ability to get everything together for a big occasion.

Don't just to listen to that inner voice, follow it.

I worked on a speech to persuade my audience that Neville Chamberlain was one of the greatest British prime ministers who ever lived. No small task. Most people don't know any more about Chamberlain than that he was an impotent practitioner of appeasement who carried an umbrella and was outwitted by Adolph Hitler. There's more to the story, of course. The problem, however, was to get the audience to remain open-minded. So I decided to lull the audience into thinking that I was talking about Winston Churchill. I would achieve this by quoting Chamberlain, but *making him sound like Churchill*. Then, when I revealed that my subject was his polar opposite, the apparently wimpy Neville Chamberlain, the audience would be compelled to listen to make sense of their own misjudgment.

In fact, Churchill had been a lifelong stammerer. He overcame his problem by crafting speeches that read like poetry—then reciting them as if they were poetry. I wanted ultimately to speak like a normal person, so if I opened my talk sounding like Churchill, I might both misdirect the audience and get off to a flying start.

British parliamentarian, Lord MacCauley said the purpose of oratory is not truth, but persuasion. The truth is that I made the facts that favored Chamberlain persuasive, and the logic unassailable—right from the opening, a Churchillian-sounding quotation, even though the words were those of Chamberlain:

> *Germany is up to her old tricks,*
> *instigating, suggesting, encouraging*
> *bloodshed and assassination,*
> *for her own self-aggrandizement*
> *and pride.*

The ending was no less cadenced. I crafted lines I hoped might wring remorse from the audience:

> *The tears of gratitude are gone however,*
> *and the years will not recall them;*
> *and this man's life, and work, and words are gone*
> *— for no man stops to hear them.*

I polished that speech, rehearsed it into a tape recorder, and recited it in the shower. Gradually, breath by breath, word by word, sentence by sentence, I crafted what I hoped was a seamless speech running almost like blank verse.

> *If you don't have a stutter, dear reader, you'll be up and running overnight. But remember—practice can be worth infinitely more than talent. The untalented person knows that success will have to come against the odds. So the will to practice is a talent, too. Have that and you'll need little else.*

In the week before I was due to give my speech, I spoke in a debate—and again came last. Some friends suggested that in fairness to myself and my club I should quit.

Then I met a sage. Ben O'Connor had won every important national speaking competition. He agreed to have me rehearse before him in his office. He said little except that I should take more time over my pauses, clearly enunciate word endings, and speak from the heart. My stutter became less and less of a problem. Finally, Ben turned to me, "This is twenty fifth year of the contest, so it will be a special turnout and the competition will be tough. But I believe you can win."

> *My experience with Ben taught me the value of enlisting the help of people wiser and more experienced than myself. So don't feel coy about seeking help. The wise mentor realizes you'll have to do it mostly on your own, and that his or her task is to render apt advice—and then depart.*

The competition, before a sell-out black-tie audience in an intimate theater, honored an airman who'd died in the Battle of Britain. I arrived in a rented tuxedo and spotted the snickering colleagues who'd given me such frank advice on my first club evening.

I'd drawn final place on the program, so I would hear all the speeches before delivering my own. A spotlit, solemn, black ribboned photo of the handsome young pilot whose name the competition honored stood on a desk on the stage. I glanced at the cue cards I'd decided not to use, then tossed them aside. I gazed at the young airman's photo, and visualized myself giving a speech to make his family proud.

I grew more confident as each speaker came and went. They weren't as well prepared as I. They seemed pressured by the occasion. They were talented and competent, but no longer eight feet tall.

Now the favored winner and second-to-last speaker rose to the stage. Tall, imposing, radiating self-confidence, he spoke in a rich, resonant voice. His polished, professional performance impressed the audience and won the best applause of the evening. He sat down confidently. He'd heard me speak on other occasions. He knew that only a miracle could save me.

> Balanchine said, "On Monday, I practice. On Tuesday, I practice. On Wednesday, I practice. On Thursday, I practice. But on Friday and Saturday, I forget about all my practicing, and I _dance_!"

Now it was my turn. I climbed the stage and gazed over the sea of faces till they settled. I stood stock still, and took a deep breath. Then, evenly and effortlessly, I began ...

The next twelve minutes seemed magical. The audience responded to my own excitement. They seemed to draw my speech from me. I seemed to become a mere vehicle for greater thoughts and feelings. My opening quote piqued attention. Then I revealed that my subject was not Churchill but Chamberlain and the astonished audience leaned forward and hung on every word. I finally exited the stage to momentary stunned silence. Then the applause began, and swelled, and continued.

The adjudicator knew nothing of my history. He critiqued each speaker in turn. Then he turned to me. He paid me many compliments, then wound up with these words, "I have placed Mister Wareham best speaker by such a wide margin that I decline to place anyone else. He is clearly a natural orator with a God-given voice."

I remembered the story of the clergyman, who, passing by the particularly beautiful home one of his brethren, commented, "God has given you a wonderful garden."

"Yes, " came the reply, "but you should have seen it when God had it on his own!"

I know all about nervousness, so I know that public speaking can seem daunting—terrifying, even. But tutoring others—from top leaders in one world to prison inmates in another—has shown me that public speaking skills are surprisingly easy to acquire. And that understanding and application can make a neophyte look like a picture perfect pro.

Let's see how.

How to Turn Nervous Energy Into Charismatic Gold

& Deliver the Presentation of Your Life

> "Fear gives sudden instincts of skill."
> —Coleridge

AFTER I WON THAT COMPETITION, people said I'd never stutter again. Yet next week the devil seemed to get hold of my tongue and I gave one of my most faltering speeches ever—and for the life of me couldn't figure out why.

The messenger who might have saved me a lot of heartache was New York researcher, Dr. Martin Schwartz. He never stuttered himself but became intrigued as to why other people did. His key insight—which had eluded every other expert in the world for a few thousand years—was that stuttering stems from a physical defect. Sure, stuttering can give a person psychological problems. But the root cause is a physical breathing anomaly—and must be addressed as such. Dr. Schwartz shows how to do so in his excellent book, *Stuttering Solved*—which I only recently got to read. What surprised me was the realization that I'd blindly discovered and applied the same insights:

◻ I'd apprehended that beyond a certain stress level, my breathing would go haywire and I'd be unable to speak. Talking to my dog would be easy, but speaking to a policeman—or an audience—would be impossible.

◻ More subtly, I'd intuited that the "background" level of stress in my life—which I used to be unaware of—was like a tide of stress. At low tide I could negotiate the waters of life without too much pain. At high tide, I was in over my head, drowning in an angry sea of bubbling syllables.

To compound these problems, the stutterer makes a classic mistake. He struggles—and struggles, and struggles—to speak. He does so for what seems a good reason: sometimes he succeeds! A sentence bursts from his jaw and he feels a rush of relief. What he fails to realize, however, is that this immediate psychic reward comes at a terrible long-term price. His habit of struggling has just been reinforced—and his stutter becomes increasingly ingrained.

Here's the moral for non-stutterers: *a similar syndrome underpins the predicament of most neophyte public speakers.*

◻ Their thinking goes haywire. The apprehension of having to deliver a speech raises the level of background stress in their lives. They suffer intense difficulty in figuring out what to say.

◻ In frustration they decide to "wing it"; or they commit some drearily portentous words to paper, then stand and attempt to *read* them.

☐ Either way, they inevitably stumble. The ultimate presentation is inferior at best—and they learn to hate public speaking. So what's the cure? Let's see.

I gradually—and unconsciously—learned to deal with my stutter by a) reducing the level of background stress in my life, b) gaining control over my breathing, and c) developing the confidence to rely on my own talents.

And that, dear reader is also the way out of the public speaking conundrum for everyone!

Let me clarify.

Lesson #1: Reduce Background Stress

The beginning of a dramatic improvement in your public speaking skills lies in six stratagems that reduce the stress of preparing a presentation.

1. Consider your goal. Your intention is to present a point of view in such a way that people will listen carefully from your first word to your last—and then remember, approve of and act upon the gist of what you had to say. This is, in fact, easier to do than it sounds, and the key to achieving it lies in two elements, *content* and *delivery*. We hear a lot of talk about *charisma*. In fact, charisma is mostly a by-product of content that is coherent and delivery that is charming. Coherence commands attention and wins the mind. Charm plucks at the strings of the heart. Let's see how we might get some of that coherence and charm going.

2. *Make your message simple.* Decide on the one major point you want to instill, with maybe three supporting arguments. Then clothe your ideas and logic with simple words like heart, home, love, children, money and freedom. If you can't find the right word go to *www.thesaurus.com*, which also has a fine dictionary. But shun jargon and ten-dollar words. You wouldn't use them on a close friend, so why toss them up to an audience?

3. *Grab attention with stories not jokes.* One of the best ways to captivate an audience is to share a story and then go on to draw a serious moral from it. The best stories, like Aesop's fables, paint vivid images in the listener's mind. Choose your words with a view to putting the listener right into the middle of the scene. Unless you're a bona fide comedian, however, don't reach for thigh-slapping gags. Any humor should flow naturally and effortlessly from the subject matter. And never try to open with a glib one-liner. It's just too risky.

4. *Prepare!* Get out a piece of paper. Write the subject of the speech across the top of the page. Beneath it, in no particular order, jot down every idea that comes to you. Don't yet try to express a whole thought. Be cryptic. When you've run out of ideas, grab a fresh piece of paper and copy across your ideas, this time arranging them into related groups. Keep on doing this until the gist of what want to say is set out neatly, concisely, and, most crucially, *logically*.

5. Identify your "hooks." A hook is a powerful idea that you sink into the listener's mind. It may be an image, a story, a line from a poem, a quote, a trend or statistic. Whatever it is, you simply make sure to plunge that harpoon into the collective consciousness. One of the best hooks ever was fired by Ronald Reagan in his presidential debate with Jimmy Carter: "Well ... there you go again!" said contender Reagan, sounding like a caring parent gently chiding a naughty child. In fact, the apparently good-natured admonition was one of Reagan's finely pointed poison darts. Nobody ever forgot it, and the belittled president never recovered.

Tossing the Ho Hum Harpoon

6. Massage your outline to fit the 'Ho-Hum' formula. The moods of an audience typically follow a four-part logic. As you stand to speak they're thinking *Ho-Hum,* so you'll need a good opening line to wake them up. Once past the Ho-Hum they'll be thinking, *So What?* So now you relate your opening line to the core of your message. Then the audience asks itself, *How does this affect me?* So tell 'em! Bring it all home. Relate your message to their lives. And now they're thinking, *What should I do now?* So, once again, you tell them exactly what to do—or think, or feel. If you'll just turn the page you'll see how it all comes together in a 3-step process developing a speech on the need for new attitudes to prison reform. There's also an All Purpose Ho-Hum Outline on page 19.

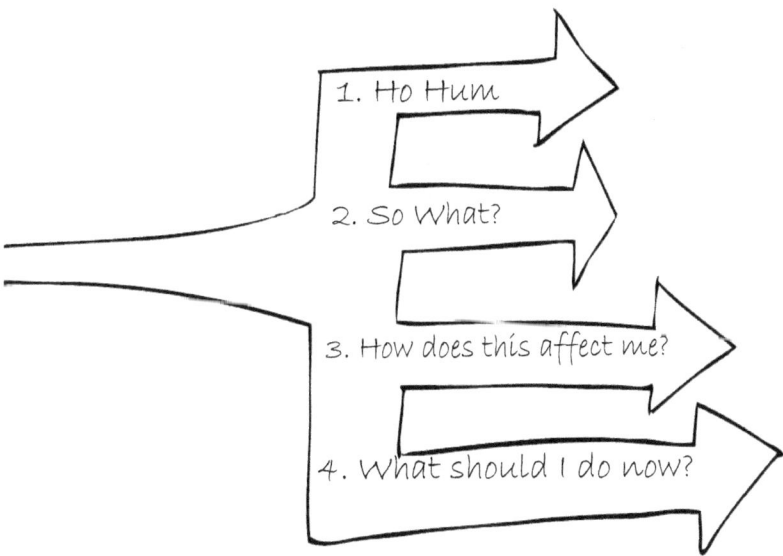

Lesson # 2: Work On Your Fluency

In my book, practice is more precious than talent. Practice is within our control, talent is not. If possible, recruit a friend to listen when you think you've got something good cooking. Practicing before an intelligent listener sharpens both content and delivery.

It can also help to write out your entire speech, and refer

STEP 1: TAP THE MIND

Deter — BUT 80% go back!
Punish → not working!
So why incarcerate? Producing more
most are
NON VIOLENT
2 mil inmates → PRISON
serve approx 8 yrs
VIOLENT
(Cure?)
"lock em up & throw away key"
no education
rehabilition
no hope!
Whole New Attitude
Nu Mission: create taxpayers!!
education
rehab
skills
shelters
Internet cafes?
↓
Get out some time! HEAD-START PROGRAMS!?
unskilled
unemployable
angry!
Might solve whole problem!
Need to Lobby congress

Step 2: Apply the Ho-Hum Structure

Ho Hum
  80% of ex-offenders return to jail -- within 6 mo's!
  2 mil inmates serve approx 8 yrs
    not working!

So What?
  "lock em up & throw away key?"
    no education/rehabilitation/hope
  They'll all get out some time!

How does this affect me?
  Will live in your community
    unskilled unemployable hungry & angry!
  Needs Whole New Attitude
    Nu Mission: create taxpayers!!
      rehabilitation / education / skills

What to do?
  Lobby your congressperson
  Demand Accountability
    Measure success of prison by # of taxpayers created!
  Donate to Eagles Foundation
  Employ an ex-offender!
    e.g. Kenny Johnson story

STEP 3: PREPARE PODIUM NOTES

THE TROUBLE WITH PRISON

- Here's the Problem
  - 80% of ex-offenders return to jail -- within 6 mo's!
  - 2 mil inmates serve approx 8 yrs
    - System not working!
- Head in the Sand Won't Fix
  - "lock em up & throw away key?"
    - no education/rehabilitation/hope
  - <u>BUT</u> they'll all get out some time!
- It's OUR problem
  - Will live in your community
    - unskilled unemployable hungry & angry!
  - Needs a Whole New Attitude
    - Nu Mission: create taxpayers!!
      - rehabilitation / education / skills
- 4 Things we can do
  1. Demand Accountability
     - Measure success of prison by # of taxpayers created!
  2. Lobby your congressperson
  3. Donate to Eagles Foundation
  4. Employ an ex-offender!
     - e.g. Kenny Johnson story

to that document in practice sessions. But unless you're a politician in command of a teleprompter, don't take that document onstage. Be a speaker, not a reader.

In the real world, you won't always have the time to write out an entire speech or to put in as much practice as you'd like. Fortunately, you don't need to. No one expects perfection. You will, however, come close to seeming perfect if you make time to do three very simple things:

1. *Write the key words from your outline, in skeleton form, on a 3" by 5" card and do your best to memorize it.* Or, if you prefer, simply scrawl that outline on the back of an envelope. That was good enough for Abraham Lincoln's Gettysburg address, so it could well work for you, too. Most of the time your brain will take over. You'll speak in your own unstilted voice—you'll sound like you —and the audience will warm to your spontaneity. If you get stuck at any point, refresh your memory by glancing at the back of that Lincolnesque envelope. The audience may mistake you for a genius.

> **The All-Purpose Outline**
>
> **Ho-hum**
>   Grabber
>   Statement of topic and purpose
>   Preview of what lies ahead
>
> **So what?**
>   First main idea
>   Supporting material
>   Second main idea
>   Supporting material
>
> **How does this affect me?**
>   In more ways than you realize
>   Example
>   Example
>
> **What should I do now?**
>   Adjust your thinking
>   Perspective realignment #1
>   Perspective realignment #2
>   Take specific action
>   Task #1 / #2

2. Craft, memorize and practice your opening. While there's no need to pen your entire speech, you should definitely memorize your first sixty or so words, for several reasons. First, it's a confidence builder. Second, since you'll almost certainly have the full attention of the audience at this precise moment, you'd be an idiot to risk squandering that opportunity. Third, this is the time to fire your finely pointed opening harpoon. And, finally, you'll never have to recover from a good start! One of the best ways to open is with a pithy quotation—which you'll likely find online.

3. Craft, memorize and practice your closing. The knowledge that you're working towards a fail-safe close—peroration, actually—is a confidence booster from the get-go. It also helps the brain to select a logical route to get you there. You'll be able to slow right down, gaze over the audience, summarize your key points, then go into your carefully practiced peroration. I often finish with a quote. Or, a telling anecdote that summarizes the need to act upon my message. And what's my message? Do the thing you most fear—which seems to be where we're headed right now.

Lesson # 3: Center Yourself

You're about to go on stage. Your hands are sweaty, your heart is racing, and you're seriously thinking about running away. What to do? Three things:

1. Grab a Zen Moment. Find a quiet corner. Block out the world. Listen to your heartbeat. Practice some very slow, very deep breathing. Feel yourself becoming centered and relaxed. Fill your lungs with oxygen now, and shallow breathing won't take the wind out of your sails later.

2. *Frame a vivid mental picture yourself giving a great speech.* Most people turn the power of mental imaging upside down. They envision things going wrong then wonder why they fail. I know that only too well. In the beginning, my 'swing thought' was don't stutter. But stuttering was on my mind so I always did. When I changed that thought to knock 'em dead the tide began to turn. So hold that powerful image as you finally mount the podium.

3. *Don't rush your opening.* Spread your 5x3 cards across the podium. Glance at them if need be to fix your opening sentence clearly in mind. But say nothing. Take a long, deep breath, gaze over the audience, and wait ... until absolutely everyone ... is totally silent. Now, *hold that pause!* Don't force *anything*. Like a dewdrop sliding from a leaf, your opening words will soon enough fall elegantly and perfectly from your lips. This will happen the moment your body begins to release

---

How to Overcome Nervousness
- Prepare!
- Memorize the opening & finishing lines.
- Practice!
- Remember, you don't have to impress—just being yourself will do
- Check out the venue & stage beforehand.
- Practice deep breathing just before going on stage.
- Trust your ability to speak unscripted; refresh yourself with "podium notes"
- Visualize yourself giving a *great* speech.
- Remember, the audience is on your side.
- Gather yourself; breathe deeply as you approach the stage.

that final deep breath. Dr. Schwartz calls this *passive air flow technique*. I discovered its power by accident. My body figured out that to speak properly I must breath properly. Unless I got off to a smooth start rough seas followed. In fact, as the Zen-masters know, breath control is the universal key to inner calm. Center yourself, and you're already half way to controlling your audience.

Lesson #4: Dance!

Now, like a dancer beginning a Viennese waltz, your words glide elegantly into the air.

The key to charm lies in simply being the real you. That's who the audience wants to meet.

Don't mumble, don't preach, don't shout, and don't try to make a big impression. *Share* your message.

Project your voice to reach the people in the back row, but speak colloquially, as you would to a friend.

Survey and speak to the entire audience, maintaining eye contact as you go.

Watch the audience's body language. If attention wanes then vary your pitch and the pace of your delivery. Never get stuck in a monotone.

Lesson # 5: Play the Empty Spaces

I was the final speaker on the hot political topic of the day, and had just finished a four-minute speech to 500 university students at a peace-rally. Those who preceded me included former United Nations leader, Sir Leslie Monroe, and several political luminaries from both sides of the aisle. As I left the stage, one of the students ran up to me. He was excited and confused. "How did you do that?!" he urgently inquired.

"Do what?"

"You didn't notice?!"

"Notice what?"

"That student audience was disrespectful. They heckled everyone—except you. Your mere presence seemed to silence them. Then you held them rapt in every word, as if on a golden thread! How can I learn to do that?"

I was nonplussed. I'd been utterly immersed in preparing and then delivering my mostly impromptu speech. I was unaware of employing any special trick or technique.

Only later did I realize what had happened. My ingrained tendency to hesitate had become a priceless gift. To control my breathing I had learned to pause—and often drop my voice—where other speakers simply sped on by. But as I became silent the audience sensed something unusual happening. They instinctively hushed and leaned forward in their chairs, anticipating wisdom. Maybe I didn't always deliver, but no matter, for at least they listened.

Now, you mightn't have a stutter, dear reader, but don't fret. The pregnant pause works magic for anyone who cares to apply it. As my dear friend, Ani Kavafian, renowned international violinist tells her Yale University master class, "It's the space between the notes that enchants the audience; that's what the real maestro knows how to play."

A related strategy following the pause is to heighten the melody—in our case the message—by coming back with a slightly different pitch and pace. Keep your eye on the audience and they'll tell you pretty well exactly when to change up or down—or when to merely keep on going.

Lesson # 6: Never Look Lost

OMIGOSH! Right in the middle of your delivery your mind's gone blank. And the audience is falling strangely silent. Well, remember this: *they know nothing*—so reveal nothing. Instead, take a calm, collected look over the upturned faces. Now repeat your last sentence. Do it slowly and listen carefully. Your own words will likely trigger your memory and get you back to where you were. If you're still lost, repeat yourself, even more slowly, and ask your audience, "What, *really*, does that line tell us? What is the message of

Common Mistakes
- Not composing oneself at the outset
- Weak opening
- No illustrative story
- Poor eye-contact
- Weak structure
- Not using own voice
- Not projecting
- Not varying pace
- Not varying pitch
- Fidgeting
- Mumbling, Umming
- Using $50 words
- Using cuss words
- Talking too long

those words?" The question is essentially rhetorical. You're merely buying time. Now, if you need to, answer your own query. Go off on a tangent if necessary, taking the audience along for the ride. You'll soon enough boomerang back on track and no one will realize you were ever lost. More likely, they'll judge you a deep and daring, stream-of-consciousness thinker. As you were, of course.

Lesson # 7: Be the Real Deal

You've transcended your fears, your speech is winding to a close, and you feel more confident than ever. That's because you know you're going to finish with a big idea. And because you took the time to memorize and hone your delivery of the precise words.

But here's a final caveat. Be confident but never self important. And never be a phony, or a pontiff, or a yokel. The way to succeed is to clothe your true thoughts with simple language, then deliver your message within the framework of your authentic personality and true self.

You can do it, I know.

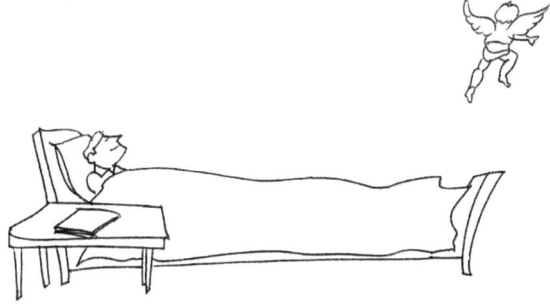

10 Steps to a Sublime PowerPoint Presentation

> "Whoever controls the images controls the culture."
> —Alan Ginsburg

PERHAPS GOD DETERMINES OUR DREAMS. Maybe that's why the words, "Create A Show" appeared on a screen at the back of my head as I lay sleeping. All I know for sure is that I took the advice and became the first executive to apply double-dissolve imaging to seminar presentations. Slide generating software appeared much later.

PowerPoint presentations have many advantages. The software helps clarify your thoughts. You can add exciting images. Slides can substitute for notes. And you can create audience handouts.

The trouble is, however, that most presenters fail to exploit the software; they merely lull their audiences to sleep. Ten stratagems can spare you this fate.

1. *Don't rely on someone else to make your slides.* I became adept in computer-generated slide creation in less than a week, and you can too. The beauty of these programs is that they don't restrict you to mere words. You can add layers, lines, circles, triangles, boxes, arrows, photographs, images, sounds, film clips—anything, really. You can create complex new slides—and sophisticated adjustments to existing ones—*en route* to the presentation platform. This is my favorite way to fill in time on a plane.

2. *Go easy on the Bullet-Points.* Most presenters mistakenly use PowerPoint to outline their presentation—and up go endless lists of cryptic, boring bullet points. An infinitely more memorable strategy is to project mind-blowing photographs and dramatic charts and graphs that illustrate your big ideas and drive home your key arguments.

3. *Build your ideas one step at a time.* I've had to sit through boardroom slide presentations where the presenter went too quickly, flashing up too many columns of figures and lovely looking charts, then dissolving everything before I had time to make out what any of it meant. The key to any presentation lies in building from the known to the unknown, and as a rule of thumb on slides, introducing words and images from left to right, and top to bottom. If I'm presenting a graph, for example, I bring it up one layer at a time. First, the X-axis, then the description of what it measures. Then the Y-axis followed by what it measures. Now, slowly, the trend line, introducing it from left to right. Now a notation on the line, telling what it shows. Finally, of course, a pithy moral or conclusion.

4. *Don't make all your slides uniform.* Slideshow programs come with templates that permit the creator of a slide show

to have a consistent "look." This is okay, but consistency can be soporific. So keep them ecstatic with a variety of layout and typography, along with apt but unusual images. Some say it's sinful for a slide to contain more than ten words. Again, this kind of rule can be deadening. In fact, I can open with a title along the top of the slide, then introduce a key idea in, say, a photo, on the left one third of the slide, then, to the right of that, a series of half a dozen or so pithy bullet points. I might even finally slap on some kind of sticker with a final summarizing point. I could end up with thirty or more words—and an audience hanging on every one of them.

5. *Make every word earn its place on the slide.* That last sentence contains nine words. I could have said, omit needless words. But that, when I put it on a slide, leaves a widow-word. Let's try, *concise and precise.* Still doesn't fit. But if I use an ampersand it will: *concise & precise.* Sometimes, an idea is too important to be condensed. In that case, I give it a slide of its own. When the creative work is done, do a practice run, making sure that the order of each slide and each layer within each slide delivers compelling, crystal-clear logic.

6. *Set up your presentation—early.* I'm ten minutes into my presentation before 150 delegates and a phone on the wall eight feet behind me rings; it's a wrong number. Five minutes later a string of profanities wafts from the public address system; walkie-talkie phones from passing trucks are breaking into my frequency. Immediately after lunch a jackhammer sounds offstage; the hotel is building a new wing. And so it goes. The bottom line, however, is that I've learned to check out everything the day before and to get the setup I need by any means necessary. When that phone continued to offend I simply tore it from the wall. I've also threatened to shatter lights that spoiled the image on my screen. There'll be time for contrition later; for the moment, my only concern is to satisfy the paying delegate.

7. *Position yourself correctly.* As you face the audience, the screen should be on your left. The reason for this is that

unless you're Chinese the human eye has been trained to read from left to right. So, after reading a line, the attention of the audience will automatically return to the presenter. Don't get stuck in one place, however. One of the beauties of the computer slideshow is that you can operate it with an infrared hand-held device. As you move around you permit the audience to adjust themselves, too.

8. *Start on time.* A punctual start says you're taking your audience seriously. There are latecomers in this world, however, so I generally begin with a story and few words that are not absolutely crucial to the theme of the day. As far as a speaking style goes, I like a natural, conversational approach—or what seems like one, anyway—but I take care to address my remarks to the back of the room, and to maintain consistent eye contact.

9. *Involve your congregation.* Before I tell the audience what I know, I like to find out what they know. One of my slides is headed *Meeting Rules.* With only that headline on the screen, I ask the audience to suggest a series of rules for a good meeting. For the benefit of hard of hearing listeners, I like to repeat every suggestion—and every question, too. I listen closely to all suggestions, then bring up my own set of rules, one at a time, leaving the audience to discover, to their surprise, that virtually all their ideas have been incorporated. Often, past experience has already permitted me to craft the layers of my slides to the precise order in which the audience is likely to offer its suggestions. Get this right and one can seem clairvoyant.

10. *Finish on time and on a high note.* I see myself as a liberator not a motivator. I aim to present an intellectual framework that someone can take home and apply to his problems. There's also a very human wish for emotional support, so I save some strong and inspiring material for the last session and wrap it up with an engrossing set of images and a soul-stirring call for action. As Andre Malraux observed, "Within this prison we can draw from ourselves images powerful enough to deny our nothingness."

And here's a final paradoxical nugget: *Don't be afraid to go out into the world naked.* PowerPoint saturated audiences can become enraptured by a presenter who can kill the projector and deliver a memorable message within the context of a cogent, hard-hitting, no-props speech. So never feel obliged to imitate the demonic herd of robotic finger-clicking presenters.

How to Give a Glorious Off-the-Cuff Speech

> "The secret of all victory
> lies in the organization of the non-obvious"
> —Spengler

THEY SAY THE BRAIN STARTS WORKING the moment you're born and never stops until you stand up to speak in public. This is especially true of the off-the-cuff or impromptu speech. Let's assume, for example, that you're attending a conference and suddenly, quite out of the blue, someone asks you to "say a few words" on the subject of the Internet—and that you have merely one minute to collect your thoughts. You're suddenly anxious and speechless. So you demur. That's the normal reaction. Yet some people turn such potential "one-minute-hells" into magic moments. They spring to their feet, tap an apparently God-given facility and issue a seemingly faultless flow of beautifully tied together ideas and words. However do they do it? More to the point, how might you? Let me share the secrets of the enthralling impromptu speech.

Most of the Magic is in the Structure

In fact, the best impromptu speeches are never impromptu. The speaker pulls a trick on the audience. As he rises to his feet, he selects a generic structure to hang his ideas and words upon. The structure provides the invisible logic that pulls the listener into and through the speech, making the speaker look like some kind of verbal sorcerer. Let me show you what I mean. Any of the following structures can be fashioned to turn the trick.

> ▫ *The 3-point numerical list.* This structure pulls unrelated ideas together. People listen closely because the brain demands to hear all three reasons. "*I have three things* (show three digits) *I'd like to say about the Internet. First,* (show one digit) *it is changing the way we do business* (expand). *Second,* (show two digits) *it's changing the way we live* (expand). *Third,* (three digits) *it's making the world homogenous* (expand)." The list can be expanded to any number, but for an impromptu speech three is enough.

- *The alphabetical list.* This structure can make the speaker seem even cleverer, viz. "I'd like to share with you the ABC of the internet. A stands for <u>altering</u> the way we live. B stands for <u>bringing</u> us a new business era. And, C, as you know, stands for <u>changing</u> the planet itself. Let me expand upon these three ideas . . . ."

- *Problem and solution.* You present the audience with an apparently daunting problem. Then, of course, you tell them how to solve it. "*The great problem with the internet is the mountain of useless data being made available. Let me cite three examples.* (Go to list structure.) *Fortunately solutions are available. Let me share them...*"

- *Past, present and future.* This is a practical all-purpose structure. "<u>In the past</u>, *when we needed information we went to the library. Or we invested in encyclopaedias. Or we subscribed to magazines.* <u>Today</u>, *as just about any school child will tell you, the information you need is sitting within the internet. Tracking that information is still relatively slow and cumbersome, of course.* <u>In the future</u> *however, in the brave new millennium, the internet will respond at lightning speed and . . .*"

- *Anecdote and moral.* Aesop made this structure famous. You simply tell a story and then go on to draw a moral from it. This almost foolproof structure provides the opportunity to tell an engaging story from one's own life, or, for that matter, anyone else's. Then, even as you're telling the story, the moral will be gestating in your head, ready to pop out when you reach the end of the tale. The audience seldom realizes that you're going to offer up a moral, so when you do proffer your insight, it comes as something of a surprise and reveals you as a reflective, thinking human being. What could be nicer?

Delivering the Impromptu Speech

Now that you appreciate the value of structure, let's consider delivery. I can offer you seven—ah, the beauty of the numerical list!—kernels of wisdom culled from personal experience.

1. *Figure out the best place from which to deliver your speech.* It might be at a speaker's lectern. If none is available then pick out a position from which you can be seen and heard with the least effort. Choosing the best spot gives you a feeling of control. You're beginning to dominate the audience even before you begin your talk. Walk slowly and confidently to that place.

2. *Collect yourself and wait for silence.* Resist that temptation to rush into your opening lines. Take a deep breath instead. As you do so fix the structure of your speech into the screen on the back of your mind, and sort out your opening line. Now, form an image of yourself giving a great speech. Now look over the audience . . . and wait . . . until everyone simmers right down. Then take another breath and—maintaining eye contact—begin . . . slowly . . . effortlessly . . .

3. *Talk about what you know.* What you have experienced and how you felt about the things that happened to you is inevitably more interesting than abstract or second-hand ideas culled from other people's lives. When you base your words upon personal experience you'll sound livelier, more confident, authentic, maybe even wise.

4. *If you get lost for words don't admit it.* You get part way into your speech and you run out of ideas—so what to do? First, don't tell anyone. As we've already noted, the audience doesn't know what's going on inside your head. Second, as mentioned, simply repeat — very slowly — the last line you uttered. *Blah de blah de blah!* Now examine the idea presented by that line. *So, ladies and gentlemen, what exactly do I mean when I say Blah de blah de blah? Well, I'll tell you. Blah de blah de blah means simply this* . . . So now go on, concocting an answer to your own question as you go. It won't much matter if what you say isn't all that logical. The audience seldom follows all that closely. Better to seem confident and assured.

5. *Take your tone from the occasion and the audience.* If it's a fun evening don't try to give a deadly serious speech. If it's a serious evening don't try to play the comic. And never, of course, try to inject 'funny' stories about race, religion, or gender-wars. Such humor can sour in a moment.

6. *Be brief. You're not the star.* Not this time anyway. If you were the luminary they'd not have asked you to speak without warning. You're merely expected to hit a theme, say a few nice words and then depart. If you get it right, people will remember you as a tactful, sensitive soul. Get it wrong and they'll call you a bore.

7. *Finish on a high note.* Don't just peter out. It's always nice to finish with a story or a quotation. One sure way to perk up an audience is slow right down, pause, gaze over the

listeners, then proffer the magic line, And in conclusion. Which leads right into my own: never forget, the audience is on your side, they want you to do well and no-one expects an impromptu speech to be perfect—so just zip that structure onto your radar screen and trust the auto-pilot to take over. You can do it, believe me.

Now that you've mastered solo speaking, let's turn to an exercise that will call upon—and hone—just about every communication skill you'll ever need to acquire.

How to Debate Like a Pro
and become an omnipotent advocate
in any setting

> "The cleverly expressed opposite
> of any generally accepted idea
> is worth a fortune to somebody."
> —F Scott Fitzgerald

PLAYING DEVIL'S ADVOCATE CAN BE REVELATORY. Most outstanding attorneys develop their persuasive skills by engaging in parliamentary debating. I was never a lawyer myself, but I sharpened my wits in debating contests with the best legal minds in my town, from both sides of the courtroom—and I admit to a sinful measure of shadenfreude in winning trophies that the local crown prosecutor did not.

A debate is a structured search for the truth—or something akin to it. Two teams, each of three speakers, lay out the arguments for and against a particular proposal, such as, for example, *That Capital Punishment Should Be Abolished.*

The various speakers lay out a case, present arguments, weigh the value of the various arguments, present rebuttals, and, finally, sum up their cases. At the close of the debate, an adjudicator pronounces the winning team, rates the speakers and explains how he reached his judgments.

The roles of each speaker

Each speaker has a special part to play. Usually there are three speakers to a team. Their various roles typically play out like this:

1st Speaker Affirmative–the leader. The leader gets the chance to define the subject. He can narrow or broaden the definition to suit the thrust of his team's case. He explains the overall case and sets out the broad headings under which each of his team-members will advance their arguments. He finally states the argument for his own broad heading. If the subject of the debate were indeed *That Capital Punishment Should Be Abolished*, the affirmative leader's speech might go something like:

> "When we say that capital punishment should be abolished we mean that it has no place in an enlightened society and that it should be removed from the laws of the land. I will show that capital punishment does not deter crime. Our second speaker will show that capital punishment brutalizes society. And our third speaker will show that having capital punishment on the statutes inevitably leads to the inadvertent killing of innocent people. Let me now prove to you that capital punishment has no deterrent effect."

Leader for the negative. The negative leader lays out his case in the same way. He might want to quibble with–or fine tune–the definition set out by the affirmative, narrowing or broadening the definition to suit the negative case. He then rebuts the arguments of the affirmative leader. He finally goes on to make the argument that he has assigned to himself. He generally devotes ninety percent of his speech to making his case and ten percent to rebutting the affirmative leader.

2nd Speaker Affirmative–Presenter. The second speaker for the affirmative generally presents the meat of his team's case. With only one speaker to rebut, he has time to develop his own special case, citing relevant examples and introducing supporting statistics. He usually devotes about eighty-percent to his own arguments and twenty percent to rebuttal. He might say something like:

> "The negative team commends and accepts the definitions given by the leader of the affirmative. To win the debate they must show that capital punishment should be *totally* abolished for *all* offences. They must prove, for example, that it is fair and reasonable to let a premeditated, vicious serial killer of innocent children live on in our midst. We on the negative team, however, will argue that capital punishment should be retained—but for specific crimes only: premeditated murder that is heinous in conception and execution. I will prove that retaining such a penalty does in fact deter certain

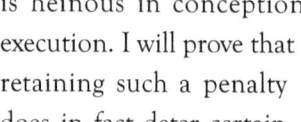

criminals. Our second speaker will show that such laws serve the cause of justice in a civilized society. Our third speaker will show that there is overwhelming public support for such laws."

2nd Speaker, Negative–Presenter. The second speaker for the negative spends a little more time on rebuttal, but also gets to lay out a solid argument for his team, including relevant supporting material. Some seventy-percent of his time will be devoted to new arguments and thirty-percent to rebuttal.

3rd Speaker, Affirmative–Rebutter. The role of the third speaker is generally to rebut - hopefully even to demolish - the opposing team's key arguments. The third speaker generally has a quick mind and wit. His skill is to spot holes in arguments, fallacies, non-sequiturs (see following

section on logic) and then point them out to the audience. He will also present a positive argument for his own side. The time split here will be approximately fifty percent new argument, and fifty percent rebuttal.

3rd Speaker Negative–Rebutter. This third speaker has the job of picking to pieces the speeches of the entire affirmative team. He can do it with logic, wit or emotion—or, ideally, all three. He must also present a positive argument for his team. Only a quarter or so of his time will be devoted to new material, the other three-quarters going to rebuttal.

Leader Summary, Negative. The leader for the negative now immediately follows. He cannot introduce new material, but can note faults in the logic of the affirmative leader's summary. He finally restates the overall logic and key arguments of his team's case.

Leader Summary, Affirmative. Now the leader for the affirmative sums up for his team. He cannot introduce new material into the debate except to rebut the argument of the 3rd speaker for the negative. He points out the fallacies in the negative arguments, then restates the strongest points and flawless logic of his team's case.

General Debating Pointers

- *Prepare!* The best debaters figure out the strongest arguments for both sides—then prepare their rebuttals in advance of the debate.

❑ *Watch the clock.* Don't waste a moment and don't go overtime. A cohesive speech within the time framework impresses audience and adjudicator alike.

❑ *Contrast your tone with the immediately preceding speaker.* If he was emotional be rational; if he was bombastic be calm; if he was dull be vital and enthusiastic; if he was a sourpuss introduce a little droll humor.

❑ *Maintain your poise.* A little irony can be effective, but anger or nastiness mostly makes the audience uncomfortable and perhaps even turn it against you. Better to seem empathetic, poised, and fully in control.

❑ *Attack faulty logic.* Don't be afraid to point out that an opponent's arguments are irrational or weak—silly, even. If your opponent makes a foolish mistake of logic, dwell on that error. Show that your counter-

arguments, by contrast, are cohesive and rational. Spotting errors of reasoning is easy, but it helps to know exactly what you're looking for. Let me show you what I mean.

Parliamentary Debate format

Affirmative	Negative
1st Speaker (Leader)	**1st Speaker (Leader)**
Define topic.	Massage topic definition.
State overall case.	State overall case.
State 3 main arguments.	State 3 main arguments.
Tell who presents each.	Tell who presents each.
Make own argument.	Rebut Affirmative Leader.
	Make own argument.
2nd Speaker (Presenter)	**2nd Speaker (Presenter)**
Rebut 1st speaker negative.	Rebut 2nd Affirmative.
Outline own argument.	Outline own argument.
Make / prove sub-points.	Make / prove sub-points.
3rd Speaker (Rebutter)	**3rd Speaker (Rebutter)**
Rebut 2nd speaker negative (maybe leader, too).	Rebut all arguments, especially 3rd Affirmative.
Outline own argument.	Outline own argument.
Make / prove sub-points.	Make / prove sub-points.
Leader	**Leader**
Expose flaw in negative presentation.	Expose flaw in affirmative presentation.

How to Seem Blessed with a Wunderkind Mind

> "Emotion has taught mankind to reason."
> —Vauvenargues

PETER POINTS THE PARENTAL DIGIT of his left hand at our debating opponents. "Their first speaker said X!" Now he pokes the feisty forefinger of his right hand. "But their second speaker contradicted him, saying Y!" He pauses. "They're utterly confused!" He shakes his head in sorrow. Then raises his voice: "They can have one or the other,"—he rat-a-tats both fingers like six-guns—"but they cannot have both!"

Pete was closing out the debate for our champion team. He pulled this trick every week, always seeming to showcase analytical genius. No surprise there, for clouded by emotion, prejudice, and pride, most people live in the land of the logically blind. The good news, however is that within that dark realm even a one-eyed man can become an emperor.

Logic is crucial to public speaking and debating. If the facts are right and the reasoning is sound you're halfway to winning the audience. The other half of the exercise lies in good presentation and in spotting the holes in your opponents' case. Let's quickly look at the seven fallacies of reasoning that they might try to sneak past you. Or, if you have a Machiavellian bent and no conscience, you might also try to slip the same set of ruses past an unsuspecting audience or opponent. But be careful. Other people are reading this book.

1. Oversimplifying the issue. Presenting too narrow a range of possibilities. "Either you are against terrorism and in favor of tough interrogation of suspected terrorists, or you are opposed to what you call torture and soft on terrorism—it's that simple!" This is a *false dilemma*. The issues are much more complex. A lot of tough-minded people oppose terrorism yet also believe that cruel interrogation dehumanizes everyone, invites our enemies to respond in kind, and, in any event, fails to gather reliable information.

2. Begging the Question. "The question is whether we can release this prisoner when he shows absolutely no capacity to fit back into society." The real issue is not whether we release the prisoner. The real issue is *whether the prisoner has learned enough to become a decent citizen*. The speaker has avoided having to prove the real allegation by assuming it to be a fact—thereby leading the audience to make the same assumption.

3. Misleading statistics. Misleading statistics never tell the whole story. "Four out of five doctors recommend the XYZ painkiller." True, maybe, but the survey was of only five doctors, four of whom were on the XYZ payroll!

4. Linking unrelated ideas. The illogical result—a non-sequitur—can seem highly plausible. Consider a rationale for the recent Iraq war: "We fight them over there so we don't have to fight them here." Sounds great but "so" is creating a false link. A logical rebuttal might have been, "We're creating enemies there—and everywhere—faster than we can kill them—there or anywhere."

5. Post hoc ergo propter hoc. A Latin phrase for "after this, therefore because of this." The fallacy lies in confusing after with because. "Local crime immediately increased when this man was paroled from jail—he is clearly to blame." Just because crime increased when the parolee was released does not mean that he committed the crimes. The conclusion simply does not follow from the premise.

 6. *Reasoning backwards.* The staple fallacy of stereotyping. "All politicians are liars. This man is a politician—and therefore a liar." Not at all. The first statement is too broad to justify the conclusion.

 7. *False analogies.* Misleading comparisons that don't hold up because the items being compared are insufficiently alike. "A criminal is like a poisonous snake. He'll always come back and bite you." Hey, what about all the ex-offenders who go on to live productive lives? Or people whose so-called crimes weren't really crimes at all—Ghandi, for example.

We could add one more fiendish ruse to this list: *abject refusal to consider the evidence.* Modern examples abound, but my favorite is the 15th century skeptic who denied the existence of the newly discovered Jupiter moons. Hoping to end the debate, Galileo, the famous astronomer, offered to share his telescope, through which those moons were clearly visible. But the cynic simply refused to look. "Those moons were unmentioned in Aristotle's treatise on astronomy," he stonewalled, "so they cannot possibly not exist." In such cases, one must highlight the devilish disregard for a) evidence and b) logic.

How to Run a Miraculous Meeting

"A good life is a series of joyful meetings."
—Francis Bacon

PEOPLE WERE SHOCKED. WHAT UNWORLDLY idiot would accept an invitation from a notorious rebel leader to run a pro-bono leadership program for New Zealand's two most demonic gangs? *Black Power* and *The Mongrel Mob* had never previously gotten together without trying to kill each other!

Black Power say they exist to advance the welfare of the indigenous Maori. The Mongrel Mob, a less idealistic mixed race gang, proudly takes its name from a magistrate who declared them "a bunch of mongrels unfit to mix with decent citizens." The warfare between the two gangs has a lot to do with carving up territory for drug sales.

A scary gathering, indeed, yet at the behest of Black Power leaders Dennis O'Reilly and Eugene Ryder—who risked their reputations to make the event happen—bleeding heart me hoped to fly in from New York, enclose them within a backwoods retreat for three days and inculcate some enlightened social consciousness. I'd get them all discussing psychology, philosophy and leadership. Big ideas would transform them. They would enter as thugs but emerge as citizens. Or so I imagined.

Cynics said they'd fail to show up. Or, if they did, they'd merely wave the middle digit and leave. Others foresaw a blood bath. Well-meaning friends said since I was doing this as an unpaid volunteer I must harbor a death wish.

I'm suddenly sharing that latter concern as thirty tattooed, leather-jacketed gang leaders swagger into a dimly lit conference room at dusk. One of their conditions for showing up is that no police be present. Effectively, the only security system is me (and my wife, Margaret, who thrives on danger).

By way of welcome a daunting dozen perform a blood-curdling Maori war chant. Then the two gangs gather on opposite sides of a semicircle. The hostility is palpable. They recline in their steel chairs, eyeing each other with uneasy disdain—then me with unvarnished skepticism. But worse is to come.

Why Bother With Meetings?

With my safety on the line, why would I ever agree to create and run such a program? Well, I was also going to stay on to present a program for a corporate client, so this was a chance to hone my skills. Boardrooms can be infested with sharks, and "team" conferences often contain backstabbers. But miracles also happen when people get together. Even among enemies, a meeting confers a sense of identity and kinship. Participants share and replenish a fund of knowledge, experience, judgment and legend—a "social mind." Tapping that intelligence increases their power. They appreciate the subtleties of a phrase. They discover the big picture, and where they fit into it. They learn the value of enlightened self-interest and teamwork. Good ideas get improved and lateral leaps follow. And, so long as they believe their views were heard and considered, people generally support group decisions—which in turn command more respect than personal dictate. The net result is that harmony replaces hostility. Or so one hopes. The gang leaders showed for similar reasons. They responded to the primal warrior call to adventure. They wanted to strut their stuff. They wanted to be taken seriously and seen to make a difference. Way down deep they wanted absolution and acceptance.

The Cardinal Opening Blunder

A meeting may have several goals, including informing, brainstorming, solving problems and making decisions. Common to all, however, one way or another, is the need to *persuade*.

Unfortunately, believing that persuasion is a matter of force, facts and logic, too many high testerone "Alpha" leaders mistakenly state their positions upfront then attempt to browbeat everyone into subjection, thereby opening the door to mutiny and mayhem. In many settings, however, nobody dares to disagree, and the Alphas prematurely congratulate themselves for inspiring and shepherding a motivated team. After the meeting, however, resentment and passive resistance set in. Nothing gets done and the frustrated Alpha impotently fumes.

The key Alpha problem is insecurity. Afraid to trust any intelligence other than their own they become digit-waving dictators. Here's what they need to know: *persuasion is a process not an event*. A one-shot hard sell might move encyclopedias but that's about it. Bear in mind too, Oscar Wilde's remark that "an idea that is not dangerous is not worthy of being called an idea." So the very best ideas are inevitably threatening. Getting people to accept them takes subtlety and skill—and begins with the agenda itself.

Where to Hide the Hidden Agenda

Some people say there shouldn't be a hidden agenda. In fact, it's okay to have a hidden agenda *so long as you hide it in plain sight.*

The agenda is a crucial piece of paper that does infinitely more than merely outline discussion topics. In fact, it typically sets a timeframe for possibly demonic arguments and emotions to be unleashed. An adroitly prepared agenda can invisibly quell those demons and channel them in the right direction. You're the anointed leader, right? So present the items to be discussed in the order that will propel the discussion towards the outcome you think you want.

Topics vary in importance and urgency but each generally addresses three questions: What's the problem? Why is it happening? How can we fix it?

Some topics unite and some divide. Open with the unifying items. Then get the trivial but urgent stuff out of the way—taking care not to fall into the trap of dwelling upon them. If there's a particularly vital item set a "time-certain". When that time rolls around, drop everything and open that discussion. A long agenda can make for a brief meeting.

Indicate the reason for each topic to be discussed. Better, for example, to amplify *Pricing Structure* to read *Pricing Structure: to consider a new two-tier pricing structure for best customers.* If possible, circulate brief—and the briefer the better—background papers.

The length of a meeting may vary, but attention flags after 90 minutes. If you need to go longer, break it up with coffee or lunch.

> *My gang-leader agenda is a bound set of background readings. It begins with the hopefully unifying idea that we are all brothers under the skin. It moves to the personal issues—such as emotional damage—that impel intelligent, well meaning people to join gangs. The final readings address the divisive issue of how an overall social structure subtly and unwittingly suppresses the rights of indigenous New Zealanders.*

Most people arrive self-certain and loathe to lose the mindset. That's why the key to changing minds is to introduce conflicting ideas and create "constructive confusion." Until we get confused, prejudice reigns. Only after confusion has been attained can clarity appear.

> *Some of the background readings were simple, and some were confusing. Most were profound, but some, though literate and plausible, were nonsense. The most powerful message lay in the overall structure of the seemingly unrelated discussions. Each reading was like one piece of a jigsaw puzzle. If I have it right we will all be guided to a bold new vision and become blood brothers. If I have it wrong, however, it will all become a bloody mess.*

Set Up for Success

The setup can also determine the outcome. So have comfortable seating and a well lit room. Crush everyone into a small space rather than address a half-empty room. And remove extra chairs to preempt the "come early and get a seat near the back" syndrome. Classroom and theater styles are fine for delivering a lecture to an essentially passive audience. Go this route if you want to retain control and keep audience participation to a minimum. If you want to get a real discussion going, however, invest in a boardroom table or arrange the chairs in a semicircle. But exercise control over where people sit. Sitting opposite one's enemy facilitates conflict whereas sitting alongside makes disagreement more difficult. Proximity to the chairman is a sign of honor so think about how you might reward or create a friend, or possibly disarm a potential enemy.

The room is somewhat larger than ideal, so I've set my hopefully soothing semicircle off to the side along a windowed wall. Each gang has gravitated to an opposite side of the semicircle, so as an opening gambit I ask two of the top leaders to mix them up. After some dragging of feet, it happens. The atmosphere seemed suddenly less daunting, and I heave a sigh of relief. But alas, too quickly ....

How to Seize and Hold Control

Alpha executives need to realize that the best way to get what they want is to surrender control. Or seem to—for the true source of power is not the barked order but the perceived commitment to a combined objective—and skill in leading the discussion to that point.

In fact, the best meetings have two leaders, *advocates* and *synthesists*. Advocates openly press for a particular point of view. Synthesists explore all points of view keep the discussion calm, logical and moving forward. Only schizophrenics can hope to play both roles simultaneously. So if you're one of those Alphas who feels compelled to fight openly for your views, let someone else run the meeting. If you'd like to get the outcome you truly want, however, then the first step is to become a synthesist. Then anoint an advocate within the crowd to make your arguments and press the discussion in the direction you think you want it to go. Or you could perhaps introduce a highly credentialed expert upfront, give him the floor to make your very best case, then include him in the discussion as a staunch defender of your secret position.

> *My Gang-Leader Agenda called for me to be introduced by Joseph Roberts, a reconstructed formerly violent felon and a key player in my New York prison program. Joe helped me establish the not-for-profit Eagles Foundation, which develops leaders from within the prison population. Joe and I had both flown in from New York. My assumption was that as a tall, handsome African American still*

bearing a few of the facial scars from his earlier life, Joe would instantly forge a special emotional connection. As the dusk began to settle outside that country hotel room, Joe stood to his full, imposing height, took a deep breath, gazed over the tattooed, arms-clenched audience, and waited for silence .... "As Malcolm X said," he intoned in a reproving yet uplifting voice, "You should want for your brother, —what – you – want – for – yourself."

Appointing another person to promote your point of view might seem Machiavellian. In fact, you're merely tossing your ideas into the arena for open examination. In your role as synthesist you'll ensure that the meeting explores all the contrary arguments. Better ideas than yours may likely surface. As a savvy leader you'll incorporate those notions into the discussion—then lead everyone, yourself included, to ultimate wisdom. Oh, yes. But before we move on, let's consider the all-time star synthesist.

Socrates wandered the streets of Athens 400 years before Christ. He never wrote a word, yet changed the world by introducing logic and reason. He professed to know nothing and confined himself to asking questions. His piercing queries created enemies and irked authorities. He was charged with leading the youth of the day astray. Given the choice of recanting his teaching or being put to death, he bid farewell with a chalice of poison hemlock.

Socratic questioning is the synthesist's secret weapon. It is a powerful tool for teachers, trouble-shooters, therapists and team-builders. It works in boardrooms, locker rooms and prison cells; with the high and mighty, the men and women in the street and the denizens of darkness. It is a slice of magic that every synthesist should be able to conjure.

It takes knowledge, intellect, and skill to use the full power of Socratic questioning to lead people to authentic understanding. It is easier to pontificate—but just not as effective. That's because, as the gods well know, we mere mortals only pay attention to the things that we discover for ourselves.

On another level, Socratic questioning is also simpler than it seems. That's because knowable relationships underlie all branches of learning. Every subject has been developed by people who shared common:

- Dreams—to reduce to goals.
- Problems—to analyze.
- Information—to sift.
- Benchmarks—to measure progress.
- Specialized concepts—to focus upon.
- Key assumptions—to work from.
- Perspectives—to provide frameworks.

Socratic synthesists question the validity of each of these elements. They act as the reasoning inner voice that the mind applies in developing critical thinking skills. The responses to their questions become like thoughts inside the mind. They must all be dealt with fully and fairly. Follow-up questions then advance the discussion, compelling the listener to apply rigorous logic. The Socratic synthesist's secret weapon is to involve everyone with open-ended questions that:

- Bring focus to the key issue.
- Examine underlying assumptions.
- Monitor the logic.
- Introduce alternative perspectives.
- Probe implications and consequences.
- Create "constructive confusion."
- Extract ultimate clarity.

Joe's introduction worked well. In the now friendlier ambience I take a moment to step into the semicircle, shake the hand of every participant, and extract a name for every face. And now it's showtime. "A life may turn on a moment," *I say, as I hoist the bound background readings.* "So what do we make of this opening quote from Dante?" *As they open their books, I read the quote aloud:*

> "In the middle of the journey of our life I came to myself within a dark wood where the straight way was lost."

"Who's Dante?" *says Kori, a Black Power warrior with a full facial tattoo and matching jade earring.*

"Why do you ask?"

"Dunno."

Long pause.

"Doesn't matter who he was," *says Coker, a Mongrel Mobber with a gold tooth* "just that he was lost."

"How come?"

"He'd gotten lost in a forest and he couldn't get out."

"What kind of forest?"

"Hey, chief, there's lots of forests in this neck of the woods."

Scattered laughter.

"Kori's right. There are many forests. But what kind of forest was Dante talking about?"

Coker breaks the silence: "The forest of the heart?"

"What kind of forest might that be?" I ask, subtly guiding the discussion to the touchy issue of emotional damage.

How to Cast Spells

A successful Socratic discussion begins with a list of questions and prior questions.

So what's a prior question?

You'd like a straight answer, dear reader—right? Okay: *a prior question is simply a question presupposed by another question.*

If someone asks, "Why do we tolerate white collar crime?" the Socratic synthesist will immediately want to settle the prior question: "What is crime?" Here comes the response: "A crime is what happens when someone breaks the law." And now the synthesist's follow-up question: "Does that apply to all laws?"

So here are the first four steps to becoming a Socratic synthesist:

- Write down the main discussion question.
- Figure out a list of prior questions.
- Do that again for each prior question.
- Stay focused on the first question on the list as well as on the last.

If you get this right, you'll create a list of questions that probe the logic of the first question. These are the questions that will underpin the upcoming discussion.

The Socratic practitioner is effectively a model of critical thinking, who asks deep, piercing questions and creates a stimulating environment where everyone is comfortable in answering honestly and fully in front of their peers—or even bitter enemies. Speaking of which ....

> *I hear but pretend to ignore a swish of doors off to my right. Two dozen more Mongrel Mobbers have belatedly decided to make their presence felt. I sneak a peek in their direction. Save for one, they are tall, intimidating and Maori. Atop their blood-red tee-shirts, they're wearing armless black leather jackets emblazoned with the face of a ferocious bulldog. Half of them are showing traditional Maori facial tattoos. Most of the others bear the bulldog image on their cheeks. Two are wearing Nazi helmets. One sports a Swastika on his forehead. Several are dragging heavy chains. It's jet black outside but many are wearing sunglasses. Catching my eye, one fellow removes his silvery shades. Or did he really? It's hard to say–some clever engraver has tattooed raccoon-like circles around the eyes. Now, fully in the room, the gang is motionless but defiant, arms akimbo. I pretend not to notice and wind down the current discussion. Then I turn to face them. Three thoughts come to mind: First, this is a higher level of depravity than I'd anticipated; second, that I'm in way, way over my head; and third, since the latecomers have the exits blocked how will we "civilians" ever get*

out of here alive? The wide and darting eyes within the discussion semicircle tell me that everyone is thinking the same thing.

One perverse way to disrupt a meeting is to engage in silent hostility. In such cases, it can be helpful to reflect upon the insight of psychologist Alfred Adler, who noted that people are mostly the opposite of the image they take the greatest trouble to project. That's why, behind the mask, clowns can be heartsick and ogres so often turn out to be marshmallows.

My stomach is churning, but with luck the Mongrel Mobbers won't notice. "Gentlemen," I say, with a big smile towards the giant who seems to be the leader, "I don't think you and I have been introduced." I stroll to the leader and offer my hand. "I'm John. I'm helping us share some ideas." He remains mute. so I grab his hand and pump it. He's still reluctant, but nothing bad has happened, so—to the horror of those in the semicircle—I goodheartedly bump his chest with my shoulder. "Didn't quite catch your name," I say," holding his stare. Long pause. "Podge," he finally mumbles. "Hey, Podge! So glad you could join us. Now let me just say hello to your friends." I coax every last one of them to shake hands with me, committing every name to memory as I go. Joseph has rustled up extra chairs.

Have you guys read much Dante?

We form them in a second semicircle behind the first and the discussion proceeds.

People judge the worth of a meeting by whether they talked and others listened. So establish some ground rules right at the outset: one person speaking at a time, everyone paying attention and no talking over anyone.

Now, as synthesist, your job is to involve everybody—and to restrain anyone who might thwart or dominate the progress of the discussion. Here are seven pointers to help you on your way.

1. In getting the conversation going, it is generally wisest to choose the soldiers first and the generals last. (Taking the bigwigs too early can inhibit the troops.) Make your questions clear and specific. Then be prepared to wait silently for 10 seconds—or more—to gather a response.

"We're talking about people getting lost in the woods. I guess that's why you guys were late, right?" Several break into sheepish smiles. *"We were thinking that maybe*

people get trapped in forests of their hearts and minds because they got harmed as kids. Did that happen to any of you guys?" Long, long silence. Intuition tells me to break my rule and confront one of the generals. "What about you, Podge?" The startled eyes of the group are telling me to stay away from Podge. He pauses. I hold his stare. "Yeah," he finally says. "You want to tell us what happened, Podge?" He twists in his chair. "I got kicked up the ass by my dad." He takes a deep breath. "It happened when I was a kid. But I deserved it. And I got over it." The atmosphere is charged. Kori breaks the silence. "I got kicked, too." The confession becomes a chorus.

2. Respond to all answers with a further question. How did you come to believe that? Do you have evidence? What are the implications? How might someone object?

"Did any of you truly ever get over getting kicked?" I ask. Podge steps into the silence. His voice is rueful. "You never do," he says, softly.

3. *No one can lead a Socratic discussion by rote.* So think along with the group as you provoke the discussion with open-ended questions and encourage the clash of ideas (but never of personalities).

4. *Listen to and contemplate each comment carefully and seriously.* Don't rate a comment until you have the meaning clear and understand the perspective it is coming from. Never rush. Give everyone time to think. Say, "Let's take a moment to think that through."

5. *Seek to understand the ultimate foundations for what is said or believed.* Treat all assertions as a connecting point to further thoughts, and all thoughts as needing development. Recognize that a thought can only exist fully in a network of connected thoughts. Shape your questions to pursue those connections.

6. *It can take courage to offer a suggestion.* And, as noted, the best ideas can seem dangerous or impractical. So welcome all suggestions warmly and give them time to germinate. And be alert for cynics who reflexively dismiss such ideas. Ask the naysayer to produce a better suggestion.

7. *Ask participants to summarize what's been said.* Then periodically summarize what has been discussed, and what might still need to be.

Finally, when the discussion has played out, and a consensus established, congratulate the congregation on their intellect and attention. Now, refine that accord into an acceptable resolution and a list of actions to be taken—noting specifically who will be responsible for each. In so doing you effectively transition from Synthesist to Advocate, with no-one noticing the switch.

As you see, the Socratic Synthesist is to the participant what the voice of critical thinking is to the individual mind. It is a voice that focuses on thinking and questions it. In discussion it is a public voice. In everyday thinking it is an inner, private voice. Eventually, the savvy Socratic Synthesist wants his colleagues to internalize this public voice. Now it becomes an inner voice that questions. Now, when they think, they question their own thoughts, bringing probing questions into the functioning of their own minds. Now they routinely think about their thinking, and routinely question the answers they discover. Now they truly have attained a higher level of consciousness.

> *We began the conference with thirty ambivalent gang leaders. Word soon got around town that something special was happening. On the final day more than a hundred truth-seekers packed that hall. At the closeout, the gangs formed two concentric circles. In the ancient tradition of the New Zealand Maori, those two circles seemed to spin as each and every gang leader shook hands, embraced, rubbed noses as a spiritual brother, then moved forward to do the same with yet another formerly deadly enemy.*

After the meeting

Never miss the opportunity to compile—or edit—a set of minutes. Sure, you'll include the time, date, venue and the names of the participants. You'll also want to mention the agenda and perhaps put your spin on what went down. (Better yours than someone else's.) Note all decisions reached and if actions were agreed upon note—and underline—the names of the responsible individuals. If possible you'll also want to include the date and time of the next meeting.

> *We were the lead item on all major television stations that night. Nothing like it had ever happened in the*

> nation's history. Next day, the New Zealand Herald formally proclaimed the outcome "a miracle."

You can be almighty, too. The magic lies in getting the right people together, setting a carefully crafted agenda into play, and taking a back seat—or seeming to, but in fact pitching the right questions (which are listed on the very next page). Get it all right and you'll soon enough have everyone singing sweetly from the same hymn book.

How to Pitch a Bewitching Question

> "It is better to know some of the questions than all of the answers."
> —James Thurber

IF YOU DON'T ASK THE RIGHT QUESTIONS, you don't get the right answers. The apt question, deftly pitched into a key moment, is a bewitching weapon. The challenge is to pose questions that initially perplex and provoke, yet ultimately lead to genuine epiphanies. Here are six ways to make that happen.

1. Keep the key issue in focus. Socratic synthesists extract clarity from complexity. Their key skill lies in the capacity to eliminate distractions and maintain focus on core issues, perhaps by asking:

How do you define that?
What is your main point?
Could you put that another way?
What is the key issue?
You seem to be saying ...
How does this relate to our issue?
Could you give me an example?
Would this be a case in point: ?
Could you explain that further?
Why do you say that?

Why always answer a question with a question?

2. Test the underlying assumptions. The road to hell is paved with faulty assumptions. To shine light into that underworld is never easy. Saints and sinners can be equally slow to acknowledge their assumptions, but these questions will help:

>What are you assuming?
>What could we assume instead?
>You seem to be assuming ...
>Do I understand you correctly?
>How might you justify taking this for granted?
>Is it always the case? Why?

3. Dig into the logic. Relatively few people are happy for obective rationality to reveal real truth. Instead they mostly use obfuscation and tortured logic to support personal self interest. That's why sincere problem-solvers ask:

>What would be an example?
>How does that apply to this case?
>What difference does that make?
>How so? Why do you say that?
>How did you reach that conclusion?
>Why do you think that is true?
>How do you know?
>Are those reasons adequate?
>What led you to that belief?
>Do you have evidence?
>But is personal belief real evidence?
>What would you say to cynics?

> What would convince you otherwise?
> Who knows if that's true? How can we find out?
> What other information do we need?
> Can someone cite supporting evidence?

4. Introduce alternate perspectives. To understand others' perpectives is also to appreciate the logic of their beliefs. It is also perhaps the most effective way to create new paradigms in all minds. These questions can help:

> Isn't this merely *your* perspective?
> Why do you choose this viewpoint?
> How might other groups respond? Why?
> What would influence them?
> How might you answer their objections?
> Does anyone see this another way?
> What are the competing arguments?
> What might be an alternative?

5. Probe implications and consequences.
It can be easier to float ideas than consider consequences. But if destiny is the name we give to our mistakes, we might create a delightful Kismet by asking:

> What are you implying by that?
> If that happened, what might also happen? Why?
> What would be the effect of that?
> Would that necessarily happen?
> What is an alternative?
> If this and this are the case,
> then what else must also be true?
> Would that outcome make sense?
> Is that the result we want?

6. Question the question itself. Badly framed queries distract, derail and deliver up nothing. Apt questions, on the other hand, maintain focus and lead us to a better place. So why not call upon the audience to examine the question itself? Like this, perhaps:

> What does this question assume?
> Why is this question important?
> How can we find out?
> How could someone settle this question?
> Is the question clear? Do we understand it?
> How hard is it to answer this question? Why?
> Would you reframe the question?
> Isn't this a leading question?
> Do we agree that this is the question?
> To answer this question, what questions would we have to answer first?
> Can we break this question down?

How to Overpower Moguls and Deliver Big-Ticket Deals

> "Rather than love, than money, than fame, give me truth. I sat at a table where rich food, fine wine and obsequious attendance were in abundance, but sincerity and truth were not; and I went away hungry from the inhospitable board."
> —Henry David Thoreau

Like Saint Peter at the Pearly Gates, most hard-nosed boardroom decisionmakers become inured to the charming words and risible ruses of even the most silver-tongued supplicants.

Indeed, in such life-altering situations such ploys and pitches may offend, backfire—or both. Hence the need for something more subtle.

One strategy favored by Ivy League graduates negotiating big-ticket deals with high and mighty moguls is *Socratic Wound and Rescue Wrestling.* You can do it do. First read this chapter. Then, next time you find yourself in a sales situation put your Socratic skills to work:

- zeroing in on the prospect's key problem,

- wounding the prospect by exposing potentially disastrous scenarios, and then,

◻ leading the prospect to rescue himself by demanding to purchase your product.

Here then, is a four-step set of jujitsu sales maneuvers to add to your communications arsenal. Apply it in those crucial big-time board room clinches. You'll surprise and overpower heavyweights everywhere.

1. *Situation questions.* First, forget polite chitchat. Slip into your Socratic mental mantle. Focus on discovering information that will give you a realistic understanding of the buyer's business circumstances. The buyer will be impressed by the professionalism of your questions. He'll be keen to help you understand the big picture. Now, armed with that knowledge, dig into the details.

2. *Problem questions.* Ask questions that reveal the problems your product can solve. If you are selling computer software, talk about updates and downtime. If you're attempting to persuade the board to use the services of your insurance brokerage firm, probe the areas likely to be of most concern. Look for risky issues insufficiently addressed. But don't get ahead of yourself by immediately presenting the benefits of your firm or product. You may fully understand the extent of the problem, but your prospect does not. Falling too quickly into a sales pitch, however well polished, will merely invite objections.

3. *Implication questions.* Don't simply blurt out the problem. Again, you'll only raise

those dreaded objections. As a Socratic synthesist, your goal is to get the prospect to see, smell, and feel the problem. Achieve this by asking questions that draw out the implications and consequences of the problem. If you ask the right questions, and then remain mute, the prospect gets to feel vulnerable, naked, embarrassed—and wounded. These are the wounds that will have them clamoring for the pills and potions available exclusively from your professional practice. But offer no counsel! Go on asking questions.

4. *Need-Payoff questions.* Ask how the wounds might be resolved. With appropriate questions your prospect

will likely ask for your product before you even describe it. The client may likely rescue himself, even before your clarify your cure. For example, find out whether any competitor was sued by an unhappy client. Better yet, have any class actions ever been brought? If so, what did it cost to mount a defense? What was the outcome? Did the jury make a substantial award against the company? Could that kind of thing lead a company to bankruptcy? Might the directors be personally liable—and in this highly sensitive post-Enron era, wind up serving jail time?

Instead of attempting to flash a light into the eyes of those whom he would save, the Socratic synthesist creates that disarming state of constructive confusion which ultimately leads others to effect their own enlightenment—then beg you to lead them to the Promised Land.

How to Turn the Devilish Delegate Into an Apostle

> "Fools can ask questions that wise men cannot answer."
> Zorba the Greek

THANK GOD IT'S FRIDAY AND THE END is nigh. I'm winding a seven city speaking tour to a close and the time by the clock on the wall behind the audience is 4.30 P.M. I'm running on autopilot, advising a group on how to fire an irredeemable employee. I suggest the "4.45 P.M. shuffle," whereby the terminee is called the chief's office late on a Friday and advised that his employment is now over. "Don't get into a discussion of why," I counsel: "Just ask the fallen fellow to clean out his desk and head home." I cite a couple of examples. There's an element of dark humor in the subject. But not everyone is amused—

"I'm shocked!" exclaims an unhappy soul in the front row. "This all so *unfair!*" How can anybody be so *callous?!*"

A burst of adrenaline jolts my spine. I terminate the autopilot and study my reproacher. He's slumped in his chair and tears are welling in his eyes.

Another tetchy voice breaks in. It's coming from the back of the room. "I'm also very disturbed, Mister Wareham," —the tone is condemning—"by both the tone and content of your advice. It's *unprofessional.*"

The room falls dead silent. A line from Shakespeare floods my mind: "When troubles come they come not single spies, but in battalions." If I don't defuse this situation they'll all be calling for my scalp. What to do?

The 5-Point Generic Solution

The time to figure out what to do with a difficult delegate is before you meet one. Here's the advice I give to myself:

- *Preempt potential trouble.* A handshake and smile can work wonders, so try to introduce yourself to everyone in the audience before ascending the podium. Once up there, toss a smile in the direction of any defensive body language. Note the back corners and the front row. Cynics favor such locations. Introduce a question-and-answer session by saying, "Some people are very shy and some people are very garrulous"—throw in a grin—"and my job is to help those at both ends of the spectrum." By so saying you politely serve notice of the need to draw out some people, and cut short others. You should also be sensitive to any potentially inflammatory material, which should be introduced with sensitivity and tact.

- *Stay above the fray.* It is not enough to "win" an argument. Indeed, it may be impossible to do so, for as the saying goes, "a man convinced against his will, is of the same opinion still." You must resolve the situation. You must transform cacophony into harmony—but without seeming to lose control. So listen closely, then deliver tactful words in the right tone. As the poet, W. M. Vories observed, "In kindness and in gentleness our speech must carry messages of hope and reach the sweetest chords."

- *Assess the personality of the apparent cynic.* Difficult delegates harbor an unmet need. You may or may not be able to fill the vacuum. Weigh their tone, demeanor, words, body language and rationality. Is the need intellectual or emotional? In my experience, heartache spurs most moaners. Agitators typically suffer low self-esteem. They're threatened by intelligence that runs counter to their beliefs. They hope to rise by bringing others down, especially someone on a podium.

▯ *Listen for the core of the criticism.* Just about all such interjections come in the form of either facts, opinions, or suggestions— so listen closely and figure out what you're dealing with. At worst, you might learn something. Embrace the cynic's perspective. Truly understand his point. Then test that understanding against your earlier words. Is it possible that the speaker is right? And that you are muddled or just plain wrong? Of course, but ...

▯ *Don't rush your response.* Praise the acuity of the question, then restate the query to the cynic's satisfaction. If you have a good answer you may either choose to give it or perhaps say that you'll be addressing that issue in detail later. If you don't have a ready answer, you might don your Socratic gown and lead everyone to a consensus. If you go this route, stay good-humored and professional. If you learn something, say so.

Implementation of the above advice will satisfy eighty percent of difficult delegates. The others may require a tad more understanding. So let's see what kinds of game these people might be playing—and then use that understanding to tilt the board in our favor.

Games Delegates Play

In his bestselling book, *Games People Play*, the urbane psychologist Eric Berne noted that people fall into and out of one of three psychological modes: parent, adult, or child. Here, briefly, is the overall idea:

> ▫ *Parent mode* communication is that of a parent correcting a child. The admonitions may be either nurturing or punitive. Nurturing parents want to help their children to grow. Punitive parents want subservient respect. Finger pointing is a feature. Parents don't like ambiguity or subtlety. They want obeisance and prompt action. Politicians often turn to parent mode. United States President Bill Clinton fell into parent mode when he wagged the parental digit and chided the naughty media, "I never had sexual relations with that woman."
>
> Smart parents also tend to respect a good idea, so if you have one don't pussyfoot around. Get to the point quickly. Cite "facts" and authority. Be firm but fair—tough, even.

☐ *Child mode* communication may be childlike or childish. Adults may become childlike when they go to parties. Unfortunately, some fully-grown humans get stuck in child mode. They seek constant childish attention. They're simultaneously idealistic and selfish. They like a happy family so long as they remain the special child. If they don't get what they want, they pout or weep or toss tantrums. So child and parent modes are complementary: the child craves attention, and the parent delights in giving it.

The way to quell children is to play the nurturing parent. Show empathy and understanding. Appeal to their idealism. Then firmly push them into adult mode.

☐ *Adult mode* is essentially analytical. Adults want to exchange information and make intelligent choices. They ask detailed questions and listen closely to the reply. They like evidence and proof. They rarely raise their voices. They want discussions to remain calm and logical.

Offer adults strong evidence and sound logic. But beware: many of them suffer "paralysis by analysis." Don't be afraid to close out the discussion. And never tangle with "the little professor", that precocious know-it-all kid who masquerades as an adult. Tell him to go read a technical text and come back later.

The way to deal with a difficult delegate is to respond in the mode that satisfies his style. If that doesn't work, summon the cavalry. Invite audience suggestions. Someone will jump in. Now don that Socratic gown again and synthesize a consensus conclusion. And don't forget to thank the difficult delegate for being the catalyst who inspired ultimate wisdom. You'll likely turn him into a lifetime fan.

So here we are again. It's Friday, 4.30 P.M. in that sweaty conference room. The tearful fellow is a wide-eyed child. He doesn't care for reality. He's expressing the opinion that life should be fair. He wants a deity to remake the world. And the scolding critic in the back row is surely a chiding parent. In his preachy opinion I need to alter my message, tone, and behavior. So now I must inject some information to show what's right—and who's in control.

"How do *you* effect a firing?" I politely ask. He's slow to respond. "Well, I, uh, in my firm we, uh, counsel employees who fail to, uh, conform to, uh, proper standards."

"And what if that doesn't work?"

"The we draw up a list of, uh, appropriate behaviors and goals—*stretch* goals."

"What if *that* doesn't work?"

"In such cases the nonconforming employee gets the message and quietly quits. So we never have to fire anyone."

"Never—wow!" I toss him a grin. "Sounds *perfect*. What does everyone else think?"

A voice sounds from the middle of the room. "We tried to go that way once. It didn't work. The fellow took the opportunity to swipe our secrets." That calm, adult voice has introduced a fact. The audience is suddenly relaxed. "Then he joined the opposition and taught them everything!" He turns and directly addresses my chiding parent. "So now we *always* do it John's way!"

"Oh, of course," responds Mr. Parent ever so sternly. "If we thought some ingrate would steal our secrets we'd show him the door in a moment!"

Hey, Mister Parent, you just switched stories!

"That's the professional way to go," I deadpan. "You use the technique sensibly, right?"

Mr. Parent nods sagely. He's oblivious to his backtracking. Didn't tag to my good-natured irony, either. No matter. Everyone else knows what happened. I turn to Mr. Child. "Can't thank you enough for spurring this important discussion. You've helped *everybody*." Mr. Child smiles wanly. Someone listened. His remarks were taken seriously. He set the world aright. He's a happy camper, now.

How to Star on Television

> "Television is for appearing on,
> not for looking at."
> —Noel Coward

I HAD HIGH HOPES BUT NO PATRONS. I was just 37 years old and my wife and I and our four kids had arrived in New York not knowing a soul. I needed to gather a following so I offered myself as a speaker to the Manhattan Rotary Club. On the day of my speech I issued a press release highlighting a key line: *executive menopause is arriving earlier.* That nugget attracted attention in the New York Times. Invitations to appear on television news programs followed. Soon enough, my firm became a key leadership consultancy.

The moral, of course, is that television can create and exalt a reputation that you can transmute into business success. If you'd like to deliver a message and enhance your own prophetability, here are my first three rules:

1. *Get known.* Include a pithy message in a press release that establishes you as an expert spokesperson in your field.

2. *Be reachable.* Provide full contact details—home, work and mobile telephone numbers and e-mail and website addresses.

3. *Be available.* Broadcasters favor those who can be relied upon to show up at short notice, so submit to interrogation whenever asked.

Let's assume your press release got picked up in the papers and now a local broadcaster is interested in talking to you. Say yes immediately, but try to get a good understanding of what you're saying yes to.

The producers will want the interview to seem spontaneous, so they won't be keen to share exact questions. But they'll also want you to make a good showing, so they'll be happy to indicate the nature of the queries.

Listen carefully to what they tell you, and if you think their inquiry won't get to the heart of the issue, politely suggest the issues that should be explored. They'll be grateful for the help.

Any relevant printed information you care to send along will also likely be appreciated. Similarly, if the subject of the interview is breaking news, you might mention that you'd like to bring yourself completely up to date, and ask to see any relevant news releases or Press Association printouts.

So now it's time to think about precisely what you'd like to say, and, most importantly, how you're going to say it. Let's deal with the latter challenge first.

HOW TO LOOK LIKE A CHARISMATIC PRO

The key to making a good impression on television, I'm sad to say, is to appreciate that television is a visual medium, so *how you look is infinitely more important than what you say!* When Richard Nixon and John Kennedy held their famous Presidential debates back 1960, radio listeners concluded that Nixon "won" the debates by virtue of logic, but television viewers agreed that Kennedy seemed infinitely more impressive. Nixon came off looking like a crook, and Kennedy seemed like the kind of guy you'd like to claim as your winning friend.

Television interviewer David Frost called television, "an invention that permits you to be entertained in your living room by people you wouldn't have in your home." In fact, however, a vital difference between presenting on the public platform and making your point on television is to appreciate that when you're on television you are effectively a guest within several million living rooms, so *aim to be a welcome companion.*

This is *not* a time to for oratorical skills. Gestures, finger-pointing and loud words will seem out of place, or even oafish—and you need to seem the exact opposite of that. You need to appear an empathetic, softly spoken, respectful visitor confidently sharing a reasoned point of view.

The late United States President Ronald Reagan was the master of this medium. Time and again, infinitely more intelligent opponents defeated him in public debate—yet when sound clips from the confrontation were aired on evening television, Reagan inevitably looked the more reasonable, charming, nice person—and viewers judged him the winner. More currently, United States Vice President Dick Cheney has the great gift of looking like a wise, charming, softly-spoken uncle, even as he advocates torture (for others, of course, not himself or his kin).

So let's think about what you can do to look like the charming, intelligent expert you undoubtedly are. Here are my suggestions.

Before the Interview

◦ *Secure an appropriate location.* If not in the studio, try to choose a location that will make you look serious and professional. If you're a lawyer, you might want to be in front of your legal bookcase. If you're a politician, you'll likely stand alongside your flag. If you're a mother who lost her child in a war of choice, you may want to take up residence outside a politician's home.

◦ *Dress the part.* You're hoping to seem like an authority figure, so your clothes should command respect. If you're a wartime leader, you might give thought to rustling up a uniform, perhaps even a flight suit. More typically, however, a blue jacket or suit will be just fine. Solid color clothing plays best on television. Don't wear clothes with patterns or lines that might look odd on the screen. Avoid wild patterned neckties and tight patterns on jackets, especially small checks. They can cause the picture to shimmer and distract. Shades of blue look great on camera and often enhance skin tones.

◦ *Be prepared to don makeup as appropriate.* Television lights can make the human skin seem washed out so the television producers will likely have you arrive in time for them to have a makeup specialist apply some tone to your face (and, if you're thinning on top, a little there, too). And those overhead lights can be hot, so keep a tissue nearby to blot away perspiration.

◦ *Remove distracting glasses.* Spectacle lenses distract by reflecting light—perhaps making you look like a refugee from a bad detective movie—so if you can get along without your eyeglasses, you might remove them for your interview.

▫ *Sweeten up.* In the course of a live interview self-proclaimed mogul Donald Trump informed CNN's Larry King, that the iconic interviewer was suffering from a particularly smelly dose halitosis. It would be unwise to emulate that, but you will want to assure yourself that your own beaming visage is marred with neither nasty odors nor nodules of spinach (or whatever).

▫ *Slow - Right - Down.* The camera reads time differently. On-camera movements—sitting, standing, or whatever—should be s l o w. To the viewer you'll seem smooth and confident (not rushed and jerky). The spaces between words are an integral part of an effective on-camera interview. On-camera time that seemed slow-motion during an interview, vanishes when viewed. So take your time and allow yourself moments to pause. But don't blink. On camera blinking is distracting and virtually compels an editor to cut away from you. If you blink immediately after making a strong point, you rob the editor—and therefore yourself—of a powerful, silent on-camera moment. And remember this: stillness is the crucial element of a powerful on-camera presence. Aim to become a candle in a windowless room—still and bright.

▫ *Conjure up a sympathetic listener.* Instead of a faceless audience—imagine you're talking to someone you know. Your tone and demeanor will be more accessible and relaxed. Choose someone to match the subject at hand. If casual, pick your best friend. If formal, choose a trusted authority figure–a parent or mentor.

▫ *Say nothing needlessly negative.* One ill-considered remark—"I love the city, just a shame about the food"—can railroad you into a dead-end station. You can wind up defending idiotic chitchat instead of nailing—or even getting to discuss—the issue you were invited to speak on.

▢ *Rehearse*. An effective way to improve your television presentation is to stage a pretend interview with a home video camera. Have someone ask you questions, then watch the tape to see how you might improve your image and demeanor. Just viewing yourself can be enlightening and comforting. First, you get to see what you're doing wrong. Then you see the dramatic improvement as you get rid of distracting mannerisms, hone your key skills, and develop confidence. Let's talk about exactly what to focus on.

During the Interview

If you've done your homework, there's no need to be intimidated by the occasion or the interviewer. Research reveals that most people are nervous in the presence of a celebrity, and, sure, many interviewers can seem somewhat exalted. But they're also mere mortals just like us. Try to see your questioner as just another friend who wants to help you to share a story. If you're nervous, say so before the interview begins. A pro will understand, and likely be experienced in putting you at ease, and keen to do just that. After all, a good interview benefits you both equally. By making you look like an expert, the reporter enhances what he hopes will be a pleasing piece of reporting. Now, here are seven key points to bear in mind.

 1. *Look at your questioner, not at the camera*—both as the questions are put and in giving your answers. Remember, you're having a conversation with an interviewer, not an audience. Sure an audience is watching, but by putting those viewers out of mind you'll feel infinitely less pressure, and

be much more natural and effective. And, of course, those parlor peekers will judge you a polite, decent, reasonable fellow, who looks like an expert on the subject at hand.

2. *Be conversational.* Be seen to share, not pontificate. If you're discussing a complicated issue, imagine you're explaining it to a new friend. Don't talk down, but don't assume prior knowledge, either.

3. *Mind your gestures.* Don't let your head bob or your arms wave wildly. The camera will usually be on a tight "head shot" so you don't want to be moving in and out of frame. If you're sitting in a swivel chair, don't swivel! Remember, too, that you've entered a million living rooms, and people get edgy when guests get overly animated.

4. *Get the name right.* If the interview is live, then by all means drop the interviewer's name a couple of times, as you might in normal conversation. If the interview is recorded, however, then you may be interviewed and videotaped by a producer who will pass the tape to the editor who creates the story, so don't use the name.

5. *Don't be afraid to second-guess yourself in a recorded interview.* If you make a mistake or slip up over a sentence, don't be afraid to offer a fresh answer. Just stop and say: "Sorry, can we do that again?" The interviewer would rather have you right than wrong, and editing sound and video is a simple task these days.

6. *Never lose your composure.* To do so is to establish yourself as a lightweight hothead, or worse. It's also a game where the stakes are stacked against you. Listeners or viewers will more likely side with the interviewer, who they already know, than with you, a relative stranger—and, if you lose your cool, an apparently uncouth interloper, too.

7. *Neutralize the Hatchet Interviewer.* Some interviewers seek to win an audience with macho machinations, and by belittling the opinions of their guests. They know the game is loaded in their favor. They want to provoke a fight. They want you to lose your temper. An effective way to deal with these devils is to envisage them sitting in their underwear, on one level, while treating them with extravagant politeness on another. So stay on surname terms. And when you're pushed, deflect feisty questions with phrases like: "That's rather unfair, Mr. Hatchett, because ..." Or, "What you're saying is kind of funny, Mr. Hatchett, because the truth of the matter is ..." Or, maybe, "Well, that sounds like a loaded question, but let me try to answer it for you."

THE MESSAGE ITSELF

"Television has raised writing to a new low".
—Samuel B. Goldwyn.

When it comes to delivering the message itself, bear in mind that television is comprised of both sound and pictures. Your audience is viewing images while attempting to make sense of sound bites—and possibly attending to domestic matters at the same time, too! The net result is that it is difficult for the viewer to follow complex answers. Seven stratagems will help you deliver a memorable message.

1. *Listen carefully to the entire question before answering.* Paying close attention to the question has a calming effect. You stop obsessing about yourself, and the brain itself kicks into gear. Now, either answer that question, or, ideally, use it as a segue to one of your key points.

2. *Keep your responses short and simple.* There's truth in the cynical observation that all television is children's television. In the age of the sound bite, if your interview is recorded, only one of your sentences is likely to be broadcast. So be brief: two or three sentences are ideal. One thought per sentence. The more thoughts per sentence, the harder it is for the listener. You can't assume prior viewer knowledge, so never use acronyms or jargon. In print, the reader has the luxury to go back and reread the passage. Not so in television.

3. *Don't signal a multiple-point answer, as for instance: "I want to make three points."*  The interviewer will likely intervene after your second point—maybe even your first—and you'll look out of control. Instead, make your points in response to two or three separate questions.

4. *Be clear on your key issues.* Include these points in your answers, no matter what the questions. As indicated, you may respond to a question very briefly, then declare, "But, of course, the real issue is …".

5. *Have command of a couple of key statistics.* Use them to substantiate your points. You'll sound informed and authoritative. Beware, though, of using more than two or three; you may end up sounding nerdy or pedantic.

6. *Emphasize your key points.* It is okay to be passionate about your subject, so try to inject a dash of 'color' into your answers, such as, "Management is holding a gun to our heads." Just be sure to have your facts straight and numbers accurate.

7. *Finish on a strong note.* In a live interview you'll often know how long you have on-air, so you can make a good guess as to when the last question is being asked. Often an interviewer will signal the close, saying: "Finally, I'd like to ask you ...". In both cases, reiterate your strongest and most central point, this time terminating your final sentence with an aptly robust word, viz: "We fight these enemies of freedom with all the resources at our command."

After the Interview

At the end of a live interview, remove any microphone you might be wearing before attempting to leave, and depart quietly, taking care to ensure an off screen exit.

As you bid adieu to face the outside world (where favor, fortune and fame will assuredly follow) thank the program producer or researcher for the opportunity to share your hard-won insights and confide that you are always prepared and procurable for such probing parleys.

Later, rerun the interview in your mind. You might even witness your words as they fall from your brain to your lips, then, with luck, out into the collective consciousness.

Don't let your inner critic beat you up with wretched

"If Only's." Call instead upon that comforting seraph who whispers, "Next Time." If there was a question you could have answered more artfully, figure an eloquent response for any future encounter.

Finally, no matter the outcome, you surely deserve praise for having the courage to put your self-esteem and reputation on the line, so the advice of writer Kurt Vonnegut Jr. might be comforting: "One of the few good things about modern times," he said, "is that if you die horribly on television, you will not have died in vain: you will have entertained us."

Ten Commandments, Two Secrets and One Dream

> "Man has power to change an unhappy condition by waving over it the wand of his word."
> —Florence Scovel Shinn

IF I REALLY AM DEAD ALREADY, it'll be okay to reveal a couple of final secrets.

First, as far as I can tell, the way to create a heaven is to select words wisely, send them out softly. The movers and shakers among the angels—and some of the devils, too, alas—are doing just that. Some of them falter, but mostly they observe the 10 Commandments of Spellbinding Speaking.

1. Thy time upon the ramparts shall be brief.
2. Thou shalt delay thy words till silence reigns.
3. Thou shalt deliver an enthralling opening line.
4. Thy message shall be uplifting, and infinitely greater than thy ego.
5. There shall be a pithy parable that thou shalt shed light upon.
6. Thou shalt not mumble, but shall proclaim with simple, soulful words and all shall hear thee.
7. Thou shalt hold thy listeners with thy gaze.
8. Thou shalt never curse or speak unkindly.
9. Thou shalt vary thy pitch and tone and pace.

10. Thy peroration shall touch the heart and linger in the mind.

Let me also confess that I've become a convert of the Jedis. We tap into the benediction of our Star-Warsian seer and sage, Obi Wan Kenobi: "May the force be with you," he likes to whisper—and in so saying softly summon the powers of the universe.

If you doubt that clout, consider this: a generation ago, just before rising to speak to a conference of chief executives. I glanced around for something to quell my nervousness. By happenstance, someone had left a Gideon bible within arms reach. I picked it up and cracked it open—and a verse jumped from the page:

> *My heart o'er flows with a goodly theme;*
> *I speak my poem before a king;*
> *My tongue is like the pen of a skilled writer."*

What a prescient thought, perfectly pitched to pacify my palpitating heart, and send me serenely to the platform.

Perhaps the universe was talking to me.

Maybe I'd tapped a kindred spirit.

The affirmation seemed so powerful that I made those lines my mantra, and they have been ever since.

As I'm sure you know, we can't always command our feelings, so imagination can run riot. We can, however, always choose our words—and by so doing bring everything else under control.

So let me invite you to become a Jedi, too. There are no initiations, no fees, no priests or potentates, no dogmas, no smells and no bells. If you'd like to tap the force, simply utter any of these magic phrases in the minutes before your big moment.

❑ *I am harmonious, poised and magnetic. My power is the power of the perfect phrase, and is irresistible.*
❑ *I tap the power of soothing words; in kindness and with graciousness my speech will carry messages of hope and reach the sweetest chords.*
❑ *All doors are open all channels are free, unerring words now come to me.*
❑ *I see clearly and speak eloquently; my words touch the hearts of all who hear them.*

And speaking of hearts, perhaps I can leave you with *Taking Wings*, a favorite poem by Chandler Haste:

> *In the dream, your heart sought the sky before*
> *you did, and started to soar of its own*
> *free will; free in the moment it foreswore*
> *the throng to fly to a fortune unknown.*
> *Inspired by that courage you followed suit,*
> *flouting the doubts of inhibiting friends,*
> *gliding past cynics in unbound pursuit*
> *of the helix your heart said ascends*
> *to the life you've been chosen to live,*
> *if only you'll simply deign to embrace*
> *the earnest pleas of that soul-starved plaintiff*
> *whose appeals you'd persistently debased*
> *—until your aching heart fled for the clouds*
> *resolved to save the only life it could.*

Dare he reveal these troublesome secrets?

A Manhattan maverick accepts an invitation to share 'a few inspiring words' with a visiting class from his former New Zealand high school, where sexual abuse was an open secret and sadistic masters ran rife. How much truth should he share?

> With unerring wisdom and dark wit, John Wareham revisits the swirling inner life of a child with a crippling stutter, whose emotional, sexual and spiritual journeys pass through rivers of despair in New Zealand, to a flood of enlightenment in New York.
>
> **"Unputdownable:** a passionate Kiwi *Catcher in the Rye*—Charles DeFanti, Kean University Professor of Literature."
> **"Brilliant and compelling** . . . reveals the mind, heart, and soul of boyhood . . . touched me deeply." Brian O'Dea, author, *HIGH: Confessions of An International Drug Smuggler*.

Welcome Rain Publishers, LLC
 New York

HOW TO BREAK OUT OF PRISON—THE JOHN WAREHAM LIFE-CHANGER

Unlock the Mind and go free now

"All prisons are mental prisons; they lock from the inside and you own the key, so only you can let yourself out."
—John Wareham

"**Invigorating**—bold ideas and an almost cocky tone combine with charm and edgy intricate logic to create a book that will result in a fresh and energized perspective."
—*Library Journal*

"**Powerful** . . . Wareham's unusual premise, readable real-life examples, and self-assessment personality quizzes will appeal to those seeking to change their lives."
—*Publishers Weekly*

"**Astonishing** . . . showcases Wareham's gift for unlocking the mind and showing us how to live the life of our deepest dreams." —**Kevin Roberts, Chief Executive, Saatchi & Saatchi**

"**A moving, life-altering work,** uniquely honed in the disparate corridors of money and power, hope, and despair." —**Howard Frank, Ph.D., Dean, Maryland Business School**

Welcome Rain Publishers, LLC

New York

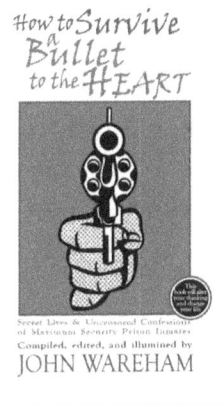

"Victims abide at both ends of a gun. Bullets fly to the heart and from the heart. Wounds that exist before the pulling of the trigger are the wellspring of crime and the font of redemption."
John Wareham,
Chairman & CEO Eagles Foundation

NEW LIVES FOR OLD.

That's the lofty mission of the Eagles Prison Program. But is that just a pipe dream? Judge for yourself as maximum security prison inmates share their journeys from innocence to criminality, arrest to bewilderment, conviction to incarceration, despair to hope, defeat to victory, vice to virtue, and lawlessness to love.

"**Blood & tears, sorrows & regrets**—every heart-stopping moment is captured & freely shared by healing desperados: I love this book." Brian O'Dea—Author, *HIGH: Confessions of an International Drug Smuggler.*

"**To pen a prison poem is to unlock the cage** along with the heart. This deft collection sparks a potent reciprocity of spirit as one harkens to the sound of wings in the night." Professor Jess Maghan—Director, Forum for Comparative Correction.

"**A life-changing anthology** —passionate and honest, ennobling and enriching." Charles DeFanti—Professor Emeritus of English, Kean University

Welcome Rain Publishers, LLC

THE PRESIDENT'S THERAPIST—THE PSYCHO-POLITICAL THRILLER
THAT APPLIES THE WAREHAM LIFE CHANGING TECHNIQUES

He had seventy-two hours to change the president and the course of history —or be killed trying.

Insurgents within the White House retain a uniquely gifted psychologist to help President George W. Bush address a clandestine addiction to alcohol and reverse the course of the Iraq War. The assignment meets with astonishing success—until foul forces come into play.

"**A winner**—a 'what-if' novel wrapped in layers of reality that offers an unnerving 'case study' of alcoholism in the White House. We enter a series of psychological and forensic intelligence forays engendered by the U.S. secret service along with a certain Dr. Mark Alter, leadership psychologist and wizard at 'coaching' CEO's into restoring their acumen and performance. In this case, however, the patient is none other than President George W. Bush."

—*Christian Science Monitor*

"**A literary and political masterpiece.**"   —*Malachy McCourt,*
Green Party candidate for governor of New York State

"**Unique, highly recommended, and sure to please . . .**
Told from the perspective of the president's psychologist, this is a story with a unique twist and perspective."

—*Midwest Reviews*

Welcome Rain Publishers, LLC
New York

CHANCEY ON TOP—WAREHAM'S WISDOM WITHIN A LOVE TRIANGLE

The price of ambition, the value of love, and the meaning of dreams

Just as his big-time dreams seem about to come true, Chandler Haste glances into the rear view mirror of the limousine bearing him across New York's Triboro Bridge, and catches the reflection of a scorching affair from his past overleaping oceans to engulf him.

"**Dazzling** . . . a delicious literary bonbon . . . —*New York Observer* "**Inspired** . . . philosophically savvy, **hilarious**, whimsical." — *Kirkus Reviews* "**Stunning** . . . an ardent . . . an affecting . . . assured exploration of moral quandaries."— *Publishers Weekly* "**Poetic gold!** The finest contemporary showcasing of the sonnet form." —Charles DeFanti, professor of literature, and author of *The Wages of Expectation; A Biography of Edward Dahlberg*. "**Shattering** . . . Those who find their wisdom in **wild and witty** packaging will love Chancey . . . **deeply moving.**" —Bernard Berkowitz, Ph.D., author of *How to Be Your Own Best Friend* "**Magnificent** . . . **racy and contentious** . . . literary and erudite . . . **profound and moving.** Captures the inner conflicts of conscience and provides **authentic insights** into the struggles of upward strivers." —Harry Levinson, clinical psychologist, Harvard Medical School

Welcome Rain Publishers, LLC
 New York

**SONNETS
FOR SINNERS**
EVERYTHING ONE
NEEDS TO KNOW
ABOUT ILLICIT LOVE
by John Wareham

America's Sweetheart

#1 Bestselling Sonnet Anthology
upon Valentine's Day release.

"**JUST IN TIME FOR VALENTINE'S DAY,** John Wareham found poetry in the lines and lies of world-class cheaters, like **Tiger Woods**, former senator **John Edwards** and **Prince Charles**, and in laments of spurned spouses like **Elizabeth Edwards** and **Princess Diana**."—*New York Daily News* "**Deliciously tempting . . . filled with passion, desire and carnal lust. . .** famous and contemporary love triangles seen from all sides."—*Ambush Magazine* "**A passionate lure** to the sonnet's delights." —David Stanford Burr, Professor of Poetry, New York University, Barnes & Noble anthologist "**Happily destined, like Milton's Paradise Lost,** to find its readers." —Don Foster, Professor of Literature, Vassar College.

Welcome Rain Publishers, LLC

www.ingramcontent.com/pod-product-compliance
Lightning Source LLC
Chambersburg PA
CBHW071717040426
42446CB00011B/2097